# DeZwaan

## THE TRUE STORY OF AMERICA'S AUTHENTIC DUTCH WINDMILL

*Alisa Crawford*

# De Zwaan

## THE TRUE STORY OF AMERICA'S AUTHENTIC DUTCH WINDMILL

FOREWORD BY MAYOR KURT D. DYKSTRA

MICHIGAN HISTORY IN-DEPTH

## Alisa Crawford

## Photographs

Front cover image by Anne Farrah.
Back cover and inside title page images of De Zwaan as it existed in Vinkel,
The Netherlands, courtesy of Stichting de Vinkelse Molen.
Other images from the collection of the city of Holland, the Holland Museum,
the Joint Archives of Holland, and other sources as listed.

Edited by Valerie van Heest.
Cover design and interior layout by Valerie van Heest.
Proofread by Ann McGlothlin Weller.

## Published

In the United States of America by In-Depth Editions, 2015
www.in-deptheditions.com
19 18 17 16 15  5  4  3  2  1
First Edition

## Publisher Cataloging-in-Publication Data

Crawford, Alisa
De zwaan: the true story of america's authentic dutch windmill
168 pages: 201 ill. Bibliography and Index (163-167)
ISBN 978-0-9801750-3-5 (pbk: alk paper)
1. Windmills  2. Michigan – Holland – History  3. Dutch History  I. Title II. Author

**2015**
621.453     2015931652

# For Diana
### 1943-2013
*For all that you were, all that you did, and the legacy you left behind*

*Diana van Kolken and Alisa Crawford*

Diana was a big supporter of the windmill and a wonderful ambassador for downtown Holland. She served many years on committees for the future of Windmill Island, and with her husband, Paul van Kolken, joined in the celebration in Muskegon when the windmill arrived in October 1964. For twenty-four years, Diana operated The Shaker Messenger, a store in Holland specializing in Shaker furniture, folk art, and Michigan-made food, and she and her husband published a magazine, *The Shaker Messenger,* that shared news about the various Shaker historic sites. She wrote the book *Introducing the Shakers* and often lectured on the subject. She had a wonderful way of making people feel welcome in her shop and always had a ready answer for visitors about the must-see sites in Holland, including De Zwaan. She was amazing and is dearly missed by many.

# Table of Contents

*Sporting a new cap and shingles in 2014, De Zwaan is ready for another fifty years of service.* Photograph by Deb Neerken.

# Foreword

Fifty years ago, a new icon began to grace the Holland, Michigan, skyline. Well, "new," I suppose, is a relative term, for the icon in this instance was the very old windmill De Zwaan. One might think it only natural—predestined even—that the last windmill permitted to leave The Netherlands would come to reside in Holland, Michigan.

As Alisa Crawford reveals, however, the real story is far more complicated, the result far less certain, the journey far more difficult than would first appear. Because of this, the history of how De Zwaan found its home in Holland is a far more interesting tale and offers insight into this industrious, diverse, and growing community.

Other American cities have windmills, and Holland had other windmills before De Zwaan. But, only at the intersection of this mill with this community did the magical story that fills the following pages emerge.

As this book was written, the finishing touches on a million-dollar restoration of De Zwaan were occurring. With a rebuilt frame, a replaced observation deck, and new exterior, this centuries-old machine looks and operates better than at almost any time in its past. So, too, its place in this community is poised to face another era. In many ways, De Zwaan is returning to its roots, transitioning from predominantly a tourist attraction to a working machine harnessing the wind to grind grain into flour. Now, as never before, De Zwaan will be viewed as it was meant to be viewed: in action.

One final point needs to be made. The author of this book, Alisa Crawford, is a vital part of De Zwaan's future. She is the miller, a title that fails to convey her accomplishment. She is among a handful of Dutch-certified millers who are female or who live outside The Netherlands; in fact, she is the only person who can lay claim to both categories. This was no simple accomplishment, for in addition to having to learn this ancient craft, she first had to learn the language—literally—because all of the instruction and examination were exclusively in Dutch.

Alisa, a Holland, Michigan, transplant who is not of Dutch ancestry, has taken it upon herself to become the caretaker of this most visible symbol of the community's Dutch roots. In this I cannot help but think of the Holland schoolteacher, Lida Rogers, another Holland transplant not of Dutch ancestry, who founded Tulip Time. That these two women are at the center of our two most important cultural institutions is a commentary about them, of course. However, it also is an unmistakable statement that this community, though closely identified in history with The Netherlands, has been, is, and will continue to be home for all kinds of people from all sorts of places.

- Mayor Kurt D. Dykstra

*De Zwaan windmill has served as Holland, Michigan's premier tourist attraction and a working grain mill ever since it was relocated from The Netherlands and opened in 1965.* Photograph by Alisa Crawford.

*The Windmill Island trademark that appears above and at the start of each chapter was selected in October 1964 from among seventy-four contest entries. Mrs. Anthony Bojarski Jr. of Wyandotte, Michigan, received a $50 award from the city of Holland for her winning entry.*

*Mayor Kurt D. Dykstra.*

# Introduction

There is no better person alive today to write the story of Holland's iconic Dutch windmill than Alisa Crawford, De Zwaan's resident miller. She holds rank as the only Dutch-certified miller in the Americas, is the only woman miller in the Ambachtelijk Korenmolenaars Gilde (the professional and traditional grainmillers guild of The Netherlands), and is among only a handful of female grainmillers in the world.

Although Alisa had an interest in history from a very young age, it was a trip with her family to Colonial Williamsburg in Virginia at age thirteen that helped her decide to make a future of living in the past. Wanting to pursue the field of history, Alisa, at fifteen, felt she needed to begin by gaining experience. Through a 4-H program, she arranged an apprenticeship at the nearby Crossroads Village, a late nineteenth-century historical village just north of Flint, Michigan. She began by interpreting the role of a teacher in a one-room schoolhouse. Interestingly enough, she was the same age as well-known author Laura Ingalls Wilder when she began her teaching career. By sixteen, Alisa was hired as a member of the summer staff at the village. She continued to soak up as much history as she could and learned more tra-ditional skills including spinning, weaving, lace-making, blacksmithing, and cooking on a wood-burning stove. One particular day has been forever etched in her mind. As she prepared to make gingersnaps on the wood stove, she looked in the cupboard in the little house and realized she needed more flour. She made her way across the village in her lace-up boots and long petticoats and entered the village's Atlas Mill, a water-powered grist mill, to get the needed flour. "The atmosphere immediately captivated me," she recalls. "The rich aroma of the grain being ground, and the white billowing cloud of flour coming out from the millstones thrilled my senses."

At that moment in the mill, she knew she wanted to learn the skills of turning grain into flour and envisioned herself becoming a miller. With a clarity rarely exhibited by adults, Alisa knew that she would have to walk a very specific path to achieve her goal, and on that day she took her first step. "Will you teach me?" she asked the miller.

At seventeen, Alisa began serving as the miller's apprentice. Two summers later, she took over when the miller left, becoming one of the first women millers in the United States. She had not yet turned twenty. However, to continue on her path

*Alisa Crawford feels quite at home at De Zwaan. She has been milling grain since she was just seventeen.* Photograph by Susan Andress.

in history, she would need a degree.

Alisa began her studies in history at Kalamazoo College in Michigan. She interned at Colonial Williamsburg, the place that had first captivated her. There, she honed her knowledge of traditional baking methods in the museum's historic foodways program. Two other internships at renowned, open-air living history museums, Old Sturbridge Village in Massachusetts and Greenfield Village in Dearborn, Michigan, plus a semester as a guest student at Berea College in Kentucky, fueled her passion.

Shortly after graduating with a bachelor of arts in history and a minor in American studies, Alisa did two things: She started a business and made plans to pursue an advanced degree. The business, called Maiden Mills, was inspired by her work in the grist mill and provided products made with traditional methods, offering old-fashioned taste, but geared for modern convenience. Her master's degree from the Cooperstown Graduate Program in History Museum Studies prepared her for a career at a museum, which, she hoped, would be an open-air museum with a working mill.

After graduation, Alisa was offered a position at Mission Houses Museum in Honolulu, Hawaii. While far from home and lacking a mill, it offered a significant stepping stone in her career. On the island of Oahu, she assisted with the restoration of an 1821 frame house—the oldest in Hawaii—and developed educational programs for the museum. After two years, longings for the mainland and the desire to live in a home of her own tugged at her. In 1997, she accepted a position as education director at the Holland Museum in Holland, Michigan, and purchased one of the city's oldest homes, a frame structure that had survived the devastating fire of 1871 and was located next door to the historic Settlers House, operated by the museum. That the city of Holland owned and operated an authentic Dutch windmill did not escape her notice.

From Alisa's first steps inside De Zwaan, the smell of the grain and flour transported her back to her days at the Atlas Mill at Crossroads Village grinding grain. After three years at the Holland Museum, that aroma became intoxicating and Alisa made a move that would change her future. But, I'll leave her to share the rest of that story in Chapter 6.

As a maritime historian, author, and museum designer, I spend most of my time with people interested in history, but I have never met anyone as passionate for preserving history as Alisa. De Zwaan is not simply a building in which she works, but a friend with whom she partners to produce flour. As the years have gone by, she has gotten to know her "friend" quite well and her relationship with the mill has grown. Her commitment to furthering her milling credentials, operating De Zwaan traditionally, conducting educational tours, and providing positive experiences for those who utilize Windmill Island for events goes significantly beyond the requirements of her job as an employee of the city of Holland.

Alisa's involvement in living history does not stop at the end of her work day. When she retreats to her historic home, she stokes her wood-burning antique Walker and Pratt cast-iron cook stove to prepare her meals and bake her tasty treats. That the stove is coincidentally a "Crawford" model delights her. In winter, she bundles up to go out back and collect enough wood to keep herself and her two young sons warm during the cold

Michigan nights. Although she drives a car, and has a refrigerator, cell phone, and computer, she hides these things in her home, preferring her stove, harp, antique furniture, and spinning wheel to take center stage.

Sometime around 2010, while hearing tales from the mill during lunch with Alisa, whom I had been friends with for a decade, I made a suggestion: "You should write a book about the mill."

Rather than answering immediately, she glanced beyond my shoulder, appearing deep in thought, and then finally replied, "I think I already have without realizing it."

She explained that as her relationship with the mill grew, she began researching its history and talking with people in both America and The Netherlands who also had intimate relationships with the mill. And she had learned some very surprising information that would change what was known about the history of De Zwaan. All she needed to do was assemble her research into a manuscript.

Together we pondered how such an icon, the only authentic Dutch windmill in America—and the subject of countless newspaper and magazine articles—had not yet been the feature of a full-length book. That day, Alisa set her mind on changing that.

As the fiftieth anniversary of De Zwaan's career in America is upon us, Alisa has achieved yet another one of her goals. This book serves to tell the true story of a quest by Carter Brown and Willard Wichers to find an authentic Dutch windmill for Holland. It also tells of the mill's career grinding grain in Vinkel, its sale to the city of Holland, its journey across the ocean, its status as a one-of-a-kind national icon, the impact its loss had on the community of Vinkel, and the many lives that it has touched, including the life of its current miller: a woman of single-minded determination whose own quest to learn the true provenance of De Zwaan has led to this book.

-*Valerie van Heest,*
*Holland-based historian and author.*

# A New Holland

**W**hen religious persecution and economic blight prompted Reverend Albertus C. van Raalte and a group of 109 followers left to seek a new life in the American Midwest in 1846, they left behind fully established communities in Het Nederland (The Netherlands, meaning lowlands) populated by some three million people. Churches, farms, and industries supplied the needs of the citizens. At that time, the country had an estimated 9,000 windmills dotting the landscape—representing an average of about two windmills per square mile—each with its own given name.

The Dutch are not credited with inventing these devices. The earliest instance of using the wind to power a machine dates to Greece in the first century. From there, the technology passed to the Middle East and on to China and India. One of the first windmills in use in what would become The Netherlands was reportedly built in 1299 in St. Oedenrode on the land of John II of Brabant (today North Brabant). It was a post mill used to grind grain, in which the entire body rotated into the wind. The technology caught on in Europe in the thirteenth century for a variety of uses. Reversing Arab technology to use a windmill to move water from rivers to irrigate fields, the Dutch began constructing hollow post, "poldermolens," in which pumping equipment sat in a stationary base, and the upper portion containing the mill gearing pivoted into the wind to pump water out of the fields (the reclaimed area known as polders). Further simplifica-

*A painting by A. Verhuell of Arnhem, Gelderland, in the mid-1800s illustrates the state of development that van Raalte and his followers left behind for life in the American wilderness. The windmills Verwachting, De Harmony, and the new De Hoop can be seen on the ridge.* Molendatabase.org.

*No book about Holland, Michigan, is complete without reference to its founder, Albertus C. van Raalte, originally from the Gelderland Province in The Netherlands.* Joint Archives of Holland.

tion led to the Dutch tower smock mills in which only the cap and sails rotated into the wind. The result was the stereotypical, four-sailed, thatch-covered tower windmill, replicated by other countries as well, but often considered uniquely "Dutch." For more than half a millennium, these machines performed a variety of tasks. They pumped water from the lowlands, reclaiming thousands of square miles for homes and farms. They supplied power for manufacturing, sawed timbers, ground corn and tobacco, and made paper, oil, and fabric.

The potato blight that began spreading throughout much of Europe in 1845, part of van Raalte's reason for leaving, had taken its toll in The Netherlands. Food and work were in short supply. Many a Dutch table also lacked meat and dairy products since those became scarce as a result of the famine. Millers were busy trying to keep the economy going, and the spinning blades of the windmills were a commonplace sight in both

*Albertus van Raalte would have been familiar with the newer De Hoop mill, built in 1846 to grind grain in his home town. Alongside a biblical reference, its name may have inspired him when he later named Hope College in Holland, Michigan. The mill has been restored as a rijksmonument (national heritage site) and today serves as a site for weddings.* Author's Collection.

the cities and countryside. In Arnhem, Gelderland, van Raalte's home town, there were many windmills, including those used to make paper, hull barley, or produce oil. The mill Verwachting (meaning expecting or anticipating), which had been built in 1820, served two of those industries. There were also several horse-powered mills, called rosmolens, for grinding grain and oats, and several water-powered grain mills in the Veluwe region near Arnhem.

Van Raalte would have most certainly been familiar with two windmills in the area near his home, both coincidently named De Hoop (meaning The Hope). The older De Hoop mill was a paltrokmolen, a sawmill that rotated on wooden rollers to turn into the wind. It had already served fifty-four years. The other De Hoop mill, built in 1846 just south of Arnhem the year van Raalte left his homeland, was a korenmolen (grain mill) built as a bergmolen (mound mill) with a rotating cap. The name "The Hope" was certainly fitting considering the mill was built to grind grain to provide nourishment at a time

*De Hoop sawmill, built in 1796 as a rotating paltrokmolen, operated in Albertus van Raalte's home town of Arnhem, The Netherlands, It burned in 1891.* Martijn Kuipers Collection from molendatabase.org.

**Chief Waukazoo was among the first native people who settled in West Michigan.** Holland Museum Archives.

**Isaac Fairbanks served as a government agent in Holland, Michigan.** Holland Museum Archives.

when food was so scarce. That mill may have served alongside a biblical reference as inspiration when van Raalte would later choose a name for a school he established to nourish the minds of young people: Hope College.

Most of the immigrants who followed van Raalte to America were not prepared for how little awaited them along the forested shore of Black Lake. The state of Michigan had only recently been established and fewer than 250,000 people lived in the entire state that comprised 96,000 square miles, as compared to the almost three million people then living in The Netherlands, only 16,000 square miles in size. The immigrants had walked into a wilderness. That is not to say there was nothing at their new home. The Ottawa Indians, under the leadership of Chief Waukazoo, had been living in the area for some time. In addition, one white family and a single man had previously settled there. Reverend George Smith, his wife, Arvilla, and their three small children arrived in 1839; he served as a missionary and after 1844 as a teacher. Isaac Fairbanks, a twenty-seven-year-old Massachusetts native, was the settlement's agricultural agent, teaching the Ottawas specific farming skills.

The Smiths opened their newly built home, called the Old Wing Mission, in late December 1846 to van Raalte and the six other members of his advance party. Poor Arvilla had spent less than a month with her husband and family in their new 24- by 38-foot home after suffering almost a decade in a drafty log cabin. Nevertheless, the Smiths could not have turned away the group of newcomers. Although Arvilla made room for them to sleep in her parlor, she insisted they prepare their own meals. The kitchen would have been in almost constant operation with people preparing meals and eating in shifts. By late February, van Raalte had built a small, crude cabin, but when more settlers arrived, they too stayed with the Smiths. For the better part of the winter, everyone struggled to coexist in the cramped conditions.

These must have been trying times for both the existing settlers and the newly arrived colonists, but van Raalte was undaunted, setting to work to build his new Eden. He played many roles to the new arrivals: preacher, doctor, businessman, and leader. Fortunately, his strength, vision, and tenacity carried him through this difficult time. He was quick to determine what elements, beyond basic food and shelter, the new colony would need to survive and thrive, including a church, a government, a general store, and a school. Construction of a church began in what is now Pilgrim Home cemetery. Van Raalte helped establish a council that met regularly and made decisions for the common good of the colony. He financed the initial inventory for a

**Arvilla Smith opened her new home, the Old Wing Mission, to the new settlers.** Holland Museum Archives.

**Reverend George Smith served as a missionary in Holland, Michigan.** Holland Museum Archives.

*The Smiths' home, the Old Wing Mission on Holland's south side, is on the National Register of Historic Places.* Holland Museum Archives.

time the orphanage was completed, there was no need for it: all of the children had been taken in by local families. Consequently, the orphanage served as a district schoolhouse. By the fall of that first year, the population of Holland and surrounding settlements had reached 1,500.

The need for proper homes for the settlers prompted immigrant Jan Rabbers to have a sawmill built, completed by the autumn of 1847 on the Black River at Groningen east of Holland. Isaac Fairbanks, the government agent for the Indians, built the mill and fabricated a dam to provide the power. In efficiency, the mill left much to be desired, and it was in constant need of repair, but willing hands kept it going until a better mill was erected. That sawmill took the form of a windmill—Holland's first windmill—fashioned after the many windmills op-

general store and acquired a boat to bring in supplies. Charitable efforts extended to building an orphanage for the children left parentless after that terrible first summer plagued by sickness and death from malaria, dysentery, and smallpox. By the

*A Holland map from 1849 shows the location of four sawmills, with the upper left circle noting the only one powered by wind. The mill on the south shore of Black Lake operated by steam power, and the other two east of Holland were likely water-powered mills considering their locations along river banks.* Holland Museum Archives.

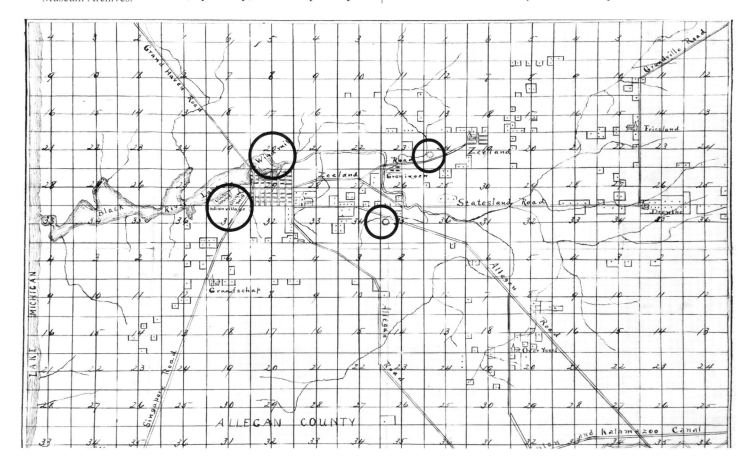

erating in The Netherlands. As the colonists had experienced in their homeland, a wind-powered sawmill allowed them to produce lumber much faster than hand sawing with pit saws. Settlers W.K. Fliestra, J. Shrader, and P. Klaver located the mill on the edge of Lake Macatawa, today at the southeast side of the River Avenue Unity Bridge. Their sawmill was operational by the spring of 1848 and provided lumber for their fellow settlers.

The eight-sided mill stood an impressive seventy feet tall with a wingspan of sixty-four feet. Its twenty-one-foot base narrowed to fourteen feet just below the cap. Wind-powered sawmills were typically equipped with a gang saw of six to eight blades, and the windmill had a potential production rate of up to 3,000 board feet of lumber per day. However, given the undependable nature of the wind, and complaints that the forests north of the lake cut off the air currents, it is unlikely this rate was often achieved. Soon, Holland's first windmill was abandoned as economically not viable. It was damaged in an August 1855 storm, and by 1870 a symbol on a local map simply listed the decaying structure as "the old mill."

In 1848 Oswald van der Sluis erected a more reliable, steam-powered sawmill west of downtown Holland at the foot of Fourth Street. The following year, he added millstones, most likely to produce flour, but his output was probably not significant. Another mill was built southeast of Holland in 1848. Though no records of it exist except a notation on a map, it was likely water-powered considering its location near the river.

Following in Van der Sluis's footsteps, Aldert Plugger, an enterprising Dutch businessman, started construction of another steam-powered sawmill in 1849, and by 1851 it was in operation. However, these mills could barely keep up with the area's timber needs. The community also was in dire need of another mill to produce flour for the growing population. In 1856 the Holland Council and other leaders held a public meeting to devise a way of securing one. According to the local newspaper *De Hollander*, "After a long time spent in the volks vergadering (people's assembly) by the doubters, in telling why a mill would not pay and the great danger from fire etc., Mr. [Aldert] Plugger finally arose and closed the meeting by saying, 'I will build the mill myself.'"

Plugger's sawmill had been a success, and he undoubtedly hoped for a similar profit from a grain mill. He built the steam-powered mill on Seventh Street on the northwest side near Mill Street. There was much anticipation about the new mill with regular updates in *De Hollander*. The December 10, 1856, issue announced, "To the happiness of all, we may inform you that the new flour mill of Plugger and Vijn will

*Aldert Plugger ran both a sawmill and a much-needed grain mill in Holland.* Holland Museum Archives.

**_Aldert Plugger's mill in Holland._**
Holland Museum Archives.

begin operations at the start of the New Year. We visited the new flour mill now being built by Messrs. Plugger and Vijn, last week. It is nearly completed. The Holland Mills will soon gain a reputation second to none."

On December 31, 1856, _De Hollander_ reported, "The new flour mill of Mr. Plugger and Co. is so far completed that yesterday and this morning we might see proofs of this."

Then, just after the new year, on January 6 the paper reported, "We saw a sample of flour which was manufactured and it cannot be excelled. Every part of the machinery seems to be of the best and most substantial character, and we boldly challenge Allegan and Ottawa counties to show a better and more convenient flour mill than the new Holland Mills." _De Hollander_ continued to describe that, "Grand Rapids people will understand that this is no idle boast, when we state that Mr. Francis Haynes planned it and with the assistance of

Mr. Ives put in the mill work; the Mc-Cray brothers furnished the gearing, an old establishment of high reputation in Utica, New York, the burr stones and their appendages, bolting cloths etc. All of the best style and latest patterns, and last but not least, that Mr. Rogers, formerly of the Sweet Mill, in Grand Rapids, is the miller."

The mill, equipped with three runs of millstones, and another used for hulling to make pearled barley, proved just as successful as the newspaper heralded, but Plugger would have little time to enjoy the fruits of his labor. He died on November 2, 1864, at age 55. By 1866, Plugger's flour mill, then run by his heirs and called The Holland Mills, was grinding wheat, corn, and buckwheat. In an inventory done at the end of that year, the mill had on hand 5,800 bushels of flour, 1,400 bushels of wheat, and 1,000 bushels of bran, along with various smaller amounts of corn, buckwheat, bags, and barrels. The total value of these items came to $4,395.50, which was quite a sum for 1866.

According to the 1870 map of Holland, two other grain mills operated at that time in addition to The Holland Mills. Pauels, Van Putten & Company operated a steam-powered sawmill and flour mill located near Sixth and Maple Streets, right on the Black Lake, and Werkman, Geerlings & Company operated the City Mills—Holland's second windmill—at Seventh Street. Hendrick Geerlings had arrived from The Netherlands in 1868, when he was about thirty-nine years old, he and his brother, Arend Geerlings, built their windmill to grind grain. However, like the wind-powered sawmill before it, his mill ceased to be economically viable. Geerlings' failure was recalled in a retrospective article in the *Holland City News* on December 22, 1910, that recognized his recent eighty-first birthday: "One of the few ventures that miller Hendrick Geerlings of this city was not successful in was grinding flour by windmill." Certainly, the inconsistency of wind might have adversely affected the production, but at just about the time he erected his windmill, styled after those in The Netherlands, the American flour milling industry began to shift from the use of traditional millstones for grinding to metal rollers. The roller mills were faster, and the process produced flour with a longer shelf life. Geerlings just couldn't compete with the

*This 1870 map of Holland illustrates the development in just two decades since Dutch immigrants colonized the area. The shaded areas show the path of destruction of the fire of 1871.* Joint Archives of Holland.

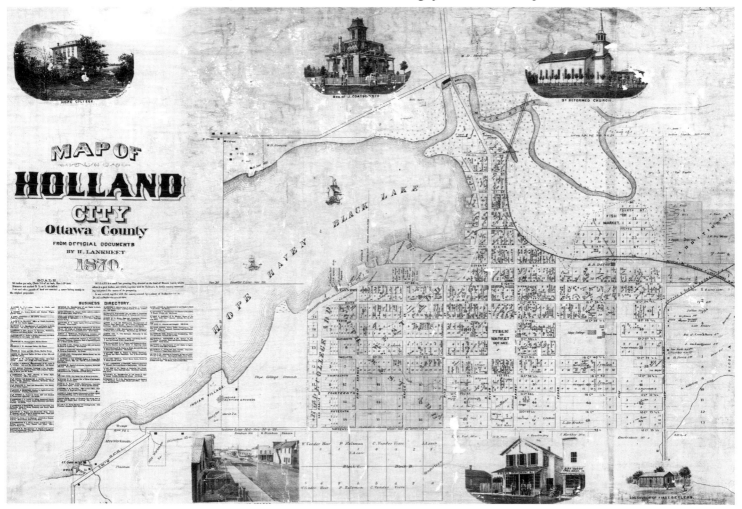

other roller mills being established in surrounding areas.

Despite these issues, by 1870, Holland had a number of thriving businesses and had shown impressive growth since the arrival of the first group of Dutch colonists in 1847, little more than two decades previous. Much of that progress, however, went up in flames during the fire of 1871, the same day that Chicago and Peshtigo, Wisconsin, burned. It began on Sunday, October 8, when Holland's founder, the Reverend Albertus van Raalte, was away preaching in Muskegon. The fire burned heavily during the wee hours of Monday morning, between 1:00 and 3:00. It is hard to imagine the panic and frantic efforts to save homes and property going on as the fire raged through the town. When it was over, 80 percent of Holland had been destroyed. Van Raalte returned to the devastation to learn that 243 houses had burned to the ground, leaving about 1,500 people without homes. In addition, 73 stores and offices, 5 churches, 15 manufacturing plants, 3 hotels, 45 barns and outbuildings, 5 docks and warehouses, 2 banks, the Post Office, and several small boats had been destroyed. Hendrick Geerlings' City Flour Mills and Flietstra & Sons Sawmill, a steam sawmill that had just also been rebuilt after it burned in 1869, both went up in flames. Fewer than 70 houses were left standing, though some businesses and other buildings survived, including Plugger's sawmill and flour mill.

Immediately following the fire, travel by train was impossible because the bridges on the north and south sides of town had been destroyed. The people of Grand Haven quickly sent supplies by boat because there was no other way into Holland. The surrounding communities began providing help as soon as roads were passable. The people of Grand Rapids sent bread, meat, bedding, and clothing. The cities of Muskegon, Kalamazoo, and Detroit provided lumber and shingles so the rebuilding process could begin. The Hollanders deeply appreciated the assistance they received, a kindness that one day they would pay forward, though they could not foresee it at the time.

By 1874, Pauels, Van Putten and Company had merged its business with the heirs of Aldert Plugger to run The Holland Mills. The December 22, 1877, *Holland City News* described the mill operation: "Since 1870 they have manufactured $140,000 worth of purchased wheat and barley. The sawmill cuts a million and a half feet of lumber, and the whole business employs some 16 hands, to whom $40,220 have been paid in wages."

However, just as Hendrick Geerlings' business had been affected by changing technology, so too was The Holland Mills. In *Memories of Colonial Life, De Hollander,* from the Van Schelven Collection at the Holland Museum, "The mill

*George P. Hummer took over his father-in-law's grain mill and developed the West Michigan Furniture Company on its land.* Holland Museum Archives.

was a good investment from the start, and it earned thousands of dollars for its owners." However, the document noted that "the day of roller process came, and it drove out the old fashioned stone mills and, among others, the [Holland] Mill was obliged to stop work." The business dissolved and the mill was sold.

Since the location of the mill was considered one of the best in the city, and the building and machinery were valuable, Aldert Plugger's son-in-law, George P. Hummer, formed a stock company and later built on that site the West Michigan Furniture Company, which became one of the largest furniture production facilities in the world.

Even though roller milling began to replace grist milling, and steam power proved more efficient than wind power for milling operations, windmills continued to play a role in the economic life of Holland. In 1881, the Holland Manufacturing Company was established to begin manufacturing the Palmer Self-Regulating Windmills,

*A wind-powered water pump, likely manufactured by the Holland Manufacturing Company, can be seen to the left of the Hotel Ottawa at Ottawa Beach on Holland's north side in this photograph taken soon after 1886.* Grand Rapids Public Library Collection.

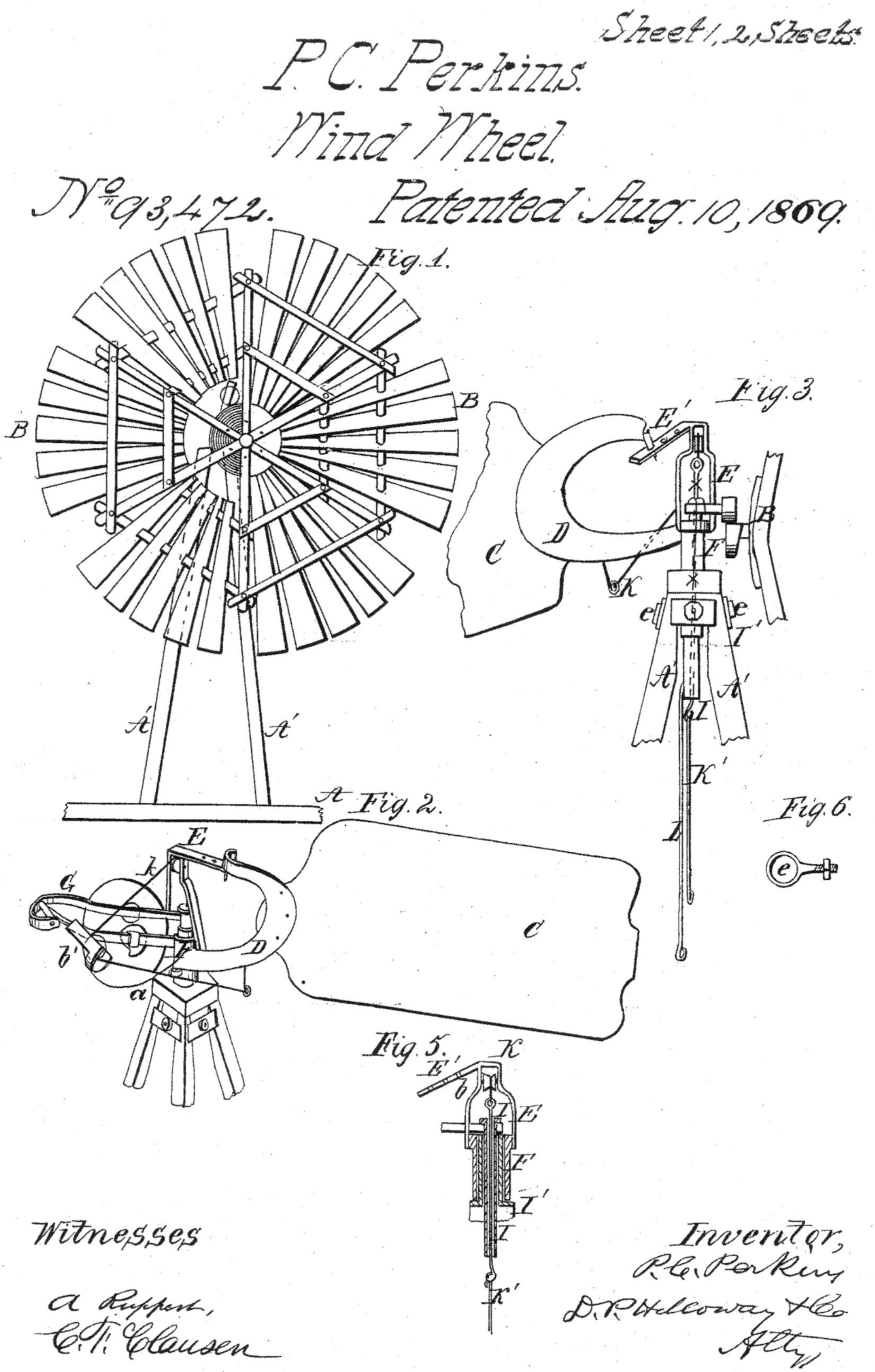

P. C. Perkins.
Wind Wheel.
Nº 93,472.    Patented Aug. 10, 1869.

Sheet 1, 2 Sheets.

Fig. 1.

Fig. 2.

Fig. 3.

Fig. 5.

Fig. 6.

Witnesses
A. Ruppert,
C. T. Clausen

Inventor,
P. C. Perkins
D. R. Holloway & Co
Atty

*The 1869 patent drawing of a Palmer Windmill indicates the type of devices built by the Holland Manufacturing Company for pumping water.* Google Patents.

small, metal windmills for pumping water, designed and patented by Palmer C Perkins in 1869. The Palmer Windmills were marketed as being durable and lightweight, and specifically boasted an offset wheel that inclined away from the wind in stronger gusts to protect the mills from possible damage. Many similar designs were being developed in that time period, and Palmer's proved quite popular.

The founders of the Holland Manufacturing Company—John Roost, Jacob Kuite, Henry D. Post, H. Walsh, J.R. Kleyn—made a shrewd business move jumping into that market at just the right time. The windmills were being used to provide water for homes, businesses, farms, and resorts, and the decade of the 1880s marked the peak production period for such devices; some 400 other firms were kept busy manufacturing and distributing windmills throughout the growing country. While wind could not guarantee the steady operation demanded by sawmills or grain mills, the Palmer mills and other similar windmills could pump water from the ground when the wind blew strong; the water would then be stored in tanks until needed. The May 8, 1886, *De Hollander* reported that, "The Holland Manufacturing Company… is expected to construct and put up fifty mills this season," a sizable order considering the company was one of many in the business. That October, the company shipped even more Palmer Windmills by railroad to Kankakee, Illinois. Business remained strong until after the turn of the century when electric water pumps became the norm.

The presence of the first wind-powered sawmill, the first wind-powered flour mill, and a windmill manufacturing company in Holland suggests that some of the early colonists drew on what was familiar from their homeland and applied that technology in their new home in America. Although the saw and grain windmills did not prove economically viable, they served as powerful reminders of what had been left behind as the settlers struggled to adapt and thrive in their new home. Many decades later, after those windmills were gone, the people of Holland would seek out another windmill to remind them of their Dutch roots.

# Operation Windmill

The seeds for what would become Holland's premier tourist attraction were planted on March 27, 1929, by an unidentified member of the Holland Exchange Club, the local branch of a national service organization founded in 1911 in Detroit, Michigan, by businessmen who wanted to "exchange" ideas on making their communities better. At that meeting, the person proposed "erecting a massive genuine Dutch windmill somewhere in Holland." In all likelihood that person was familiar with the authentic Dutch windmill that had recently been exported for an estate in Kalamazoo County.

In 1925, Will Keith Kellogg, founder of the Kellogg Company, breakfast cereal makers, began planning an estate on Gull Lake not far from Battle Creek, Michigan, the location of his factory and offices. He hired the architectural firm Benjamin & Benjamin of Grand Rapids to design it. The firm developed a plan for a Tudor-style country estate, including a manor house, boathouse, pergola, dock, pump house, caretaker's house, greenhouse, gardener's building and tool shed, storage house, a garage with chauffeur's residence, a stable for horses, chickens, and other animals, and Dutch gardens, including a windmill.

*Poldermolen 259 as it appeared on W. K. Kellogg's estate in 1927. It had thatch siding, the most common material on windmills in The Netherlands.* From *W. K. Kellogg and His Gull Lake Home* by Linda Oliphant Stanford.

From the correspondence between Kellogg and architect Adrian Benjamin, it is clear that the idea for the windmill was the architect's, as a part of the overall plan for the estate. He tried to be persuasive when he wrote in a letter on August 17, 1926, to Kellogg, "To my mind nothing would be more fitting for the island than a Dutch windmill and a tulip garden, and the thought has come to me several times that it would be more appropriate to get a real mill from Holland and erect it on your estate." As inducement, he added, "I noted in a recent architectural magazine that the owner of an estate on Long Island had just erected a mill on his grounds that he purchased in Holland. I thought that maybe the quaintness and novelty of having the real mill on your island would appeal to you."

Records do not survive of what mill that might have been, but in addition to that imported mill there were many American-made windmills on Long Island, and several had been relocated to estates. The 1810-built Shelter Island Windmill was moved in 1926 to Sylvester Manor, and the 1813-built Wainscott Windmill was moved in 1922 to an estate in the exclusive Georgica Association in East Hampton.

Kellogg responded to his architect's suggestion, saying, "I doubt the advis-

*Poldermolen 259 as it appeared in Heeg, Friesland, The Netherlands, before being dismantled and shipped to Holland. The parts of a second mill were also sent in order to be used in the restoration.* P. Hofkamp Collection molendatabase.org

ability of bringing over a large mill from Holland at any price, as my recollection is that thcse mills are very large cumbersome affairs. If you will talk this over with some Hollander who is familiar with the mills in Holland, I think he will confirm what I have said."

Despite Kellogg's concerns, Adrian Benjamin continued to push his windmill concept, perhaps due to his own aesthetic sensibilities, and finally Kellogg agreed. In January 1927, Benjamin began negotiations for a windmill with D. Woudstra from Ijlst in the province of Friesland. The architect had a friend, Peter Vander Laan, handle the negotiations by visiting Woudstra in The Netherlands. He learned there that "a windmill could be purchased for approximately $100, the total cost being approximately $650 including delivery to New York."

The chosen mill was owned by Mebius Hettinga from a town called Heeg near Ijlst in Southwest Friesland. It was a small, eight-sided poldermolen (water-pumping mill) of a type typical in Friesland called a "monniksmolen," covered in thatch. Unlike most windmills in The Netherlands, it had no name, just Polder 259, typical of the numerous, small water-pumping windmills in Friesland.

In mid-February that year, Benjamin purchased the windmill from Woudstra and arranged to have it disassembled and sent to Michigan. In early June 1927, Woudstra reported, "We tell you that we are very much occupied with your mill. It is very difficult to take an old mill down, different parts are too old or broken, for which we make new parts. Therefore we have bought a second mill, just like yours and from these two mills, we are making one good one for you. All things that are inferior, we make new.

We understand that you know that all these mills are about 100 years old, so that there is much to bring in order."

The other mill was Polder 261, which stood very close to Polder 259, as the number suggests. It had been built around 1832, and was named Molen van de Flappers after the miller who had it relocated to Heeg in 1897.

When the hybrid windmill was erected on Kellogg's estate at Gull Lake later in 1927, it was thatched, had white and brightly colored latticework covered in part with canvas sails, and actually pumped water through the lagoon via an Archimedean screw inside the mill.

Two years later, the Holland Exchange Club's publication, *The Windmill*, outlined the proposal for a Dutch windmill for Holland in a spring 1929 issue:

*...a member of the Exchange Club advocated that Holland should import a genuine Dutch windmill and erect it, perhaps in Kollen Memorial Park as a token of Holland's distinctive character among American cities. The Dutch windmill is a universal emblem. It is known the world over. It is an integral part of a great tradition. It is a subject for great artists. It has become an object of great solicitation lest the modern mechanical age destroy the windmills of Holland. A society for their protection has been organized. Would it not be a fine thing if, instead of the many little Dutchisms on our streets, we should have a great mill with its wing span of eighty feet towering over the city and looking toward the harbor of this future ocean port? It would become a place of pilgrimage for tourists that would rival any attractions in Western Michigan. It would be a fine tribute by a city with a great future to a people with a great tradition.*

Just one year earlier, Lida Rogers, a biology teacher at Holland High School, made a different suggestion to honor the tradition of the city's forefathers. During a lecture she entitled "Civic Beauty" and presented to the members of the Women's Literary Club on April 26, 1927, she spoke at length about the area's unique sand dunes, its fine trees, safe water supply, pure milk, and ample playgrounds. Knowing that the local Chamber of Commerce had been seeking something appropriate to advertise the city, she told the women, "I think I have something in mind that will do it, but I would do it not for the sake of advertising, but to add to the beauty of our city and make people want to live here." Her idea was the tulip, a symbol of the Dutch. She envisioned her biology department launching a campaign to plant tulips in every park and yard and "setting aside one day each year as Tulip Day." She concluded her talk by reading a specific stanza of the poem "The Barrel-Organ" by English poet Alfred Noyes, substituting certain words (as marked) to give the poem a more local spin. Her word choice would give rise to a festival that has endured for more than eight decades.

*Come down to ~~Kew~~ **Holland** in ~~lilac~~ **tulip**-time, in ~~lilac~~ **tulip**-time, in ~~lilac~~ **tulip**-time;*
*Come down to ~~Kew~~ **Holland** in ~~lilac~~ **tulip**-time, (it isn't far ~~from London~~ **to go**!)*
*And you shall wander hand in hand with love in summer's wonderland;*
*Come down to ~~Kew~~ **Holland** in ~~lilac~~ **tulip**-time, (it isn't far ~~from London~~ **to go**!)*

The Holland City Council supported Lida Rogers' suggestion. After some discussion, the council, under the leadership of Mayor Ernest C. Brooks, appropriated funds in 1928 to import 100,000 tulip

*Lida Rogers proposed an idea to plant tulips and celebrate Holland's Dutch heritage with a festival. Her idea resulted in Tulip Time, an annual spring festival held since 1929.* Joint Archives of Holland.

bulbs from The Netherlands, which were planted in city parks and made available to Holland residents for one penny each. A group of twelve men, dubbed the Minute Men's Club, led by Brooks, laid plans for a "Tulip Day" the following year, scheduled for a Saturday in mid-May when the tulips would be in full

*The Windmill Gas Station, built in the 1920s along the West Michigan Pike at the corner of 64th St. and Division St. (now 32nd St.), employed a pseudo-windmill to serve as its icon. It represents the first known attempt in the twentieth century to link the city with its Dutch roots.* Joint Archives of Holland.

blossom. The event proved a success: Thousands of tourists visited the city in May 1929 and marveled at the beautiful blooms.

So many people came to see the tulips that the city decided to make the event an annual festival called, as Lida Rogers first coined, "Tulip Time." Mrs. Ethel Telling accepted the role as the chairman, and under her leadership the next festival included the participation of people in Dutch costumes and wooden shoes, highlighting old Netherlands' customs and traditions.

"TULIP REIGNS AS QUEEN IN CITY," boasted *The Holland Evening Sentinel* on May 12, 1930, to inaugurate the four-day festival that included a flower show, a high school operetta, and a combined band concert. In 1931, the festival ran from May 15 to May 22, and attracted many more thousands of people to the city.

In 1933 the first Tulip Time office opened, incorporating festival management with the Chamber of Commerce. That year, Esther Perry, a high school girls' gym teacher, trained the Dutch Villagers, later known as Klompen Dancers, to perform Dutch folk dances. Twelve

dancers performed that year to the song "Where, Oh Where, Has My Little Dog Gone?"

In 1934 Holland Chamber of Commerce Manager William Connelly and Park Superintendent John Van Bragt directed construction of a replica windmill in the swampland near the River Avenue bridge (today known as the Unity Bridge). It was patterned after the twenty-foot-high Dutch water mill that had recently been erected on the grounds of cereal magnate W. K. Kellogg's new estate on Gull Lake. The park, first called Lakeview Park, and later Windmill Park (now Van Bragt Park) served as a tulip bed for the annual festival.

By the mid-1930s, Tulip Time had become a nationally known event that took place over nine days. In 1935, the festival boasted a feature attraction: a miniature village called "Klein Nederland" (Little Netherlands) depicting the rural life of Holland's founding fathers several centuries earlier. The village was initially displayed in the Holland Armory.

Tulip Time's tourist draw prompted the Nelis family, local farmers, to purchase eighty acres north of Holland and

WIND MILL PARK HOLLAND MICH.          J-304

*A small, replica windmill, modeled after the Dutch windmill purchased by W. K. Kellogg, was erected in 1934 along the Black Lake shore, and still stands today in what is now known as Van Bragt Park, named after the man who helped place the windmill there.* Joint Archives of Holland.

The committee used the May 1940 Tulip Time celebration as a platform to appeal for donations. Citizens also organized "Netherlands' Day" in Centennial Park in Holland on May 22 that year. The two initiatives raised over $5,000, a good first effort.

News of deteriorating living conditions in The Netherlands reached the people of Holland. The Dutch, they learned, were being compelled to join the Nazi party, civilians were drafted for forced labor, homes along the Atlantic coast were seized for defensive positions, Dutch Jews were rounded up and

*Nelis' Dutch Village planted extensive fields of tulips and built a small, replica Dutch windmill. The village remains a popular attraction today.* Joint Archives of Holland.

*"Klein Nederland" (Little Netherlands), a miniature village, was among early projects to honor the area's Dutch roots. It is currently on display at Windmill Island.* Holland Museum Archives.

go into the nursery business. They planted thousands of tulip bulbs and constructed a scaled-down windmill on the property to cultivate the Dutch theme. By the late 1930s, Nelis' Dutch Village became a main attraction for Tulip Time visitors.

War erupting in Europe in the fall of 1939 and the German invasion of The Netherlands in April 1940 changed the tone of the festival. Rather than celebrate Dutch roots, Hollanders instead did all they could to help their fellow Dutchmen in The Netherlands, just as they themselves had been helped after the tragic fire in 1871. Holland's mayor Henry Geerlings, whose parents hailed from The Netherlands, immediately set up a committee to develop a relief fund.

sent to concentration camps, and food was rationed. Willard C. Wichers, a second-generation Dutch-American, set up in 1940 the Queen Wilhelmina Fund, earmarking donations to assist the Dutch after the war.

Born in Zeeland, Michigan, on March 20, 1909, to Henry Wichers and

*Willard C. Wichers led a fund-raising campaign during World War II to help the people suffering in The Netherlands. The embossed tile and barrel-organ were later given to Holland, Michigan, in appreciation, and are on display at Windmill Island.* Holland Museum Archives.

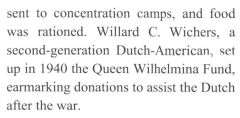

Mamie Vrieling Wichers, Wichers attended the public schools and majored in chemistry at Hope College and later at the University of Michigan. He married Nell Elizabeth Van Haitsma in 1937, and they had two daughters, Elizabeth and Janet. Wichers began his career working as a night chemist at the sugar beet factory in Holland. On the side, he set up a small public relations business, and later became the West Michigan supervisor of the Historical Records Survey Project. He felt very strongly about the importance of history and joined many historical organizations, including the Holland Historical Cultural Commission, Holland Area Historical Advisory Commission, Michigan Historic Preservation Review Board, Historical Society of Michigan, and Netherlands Pioneer and Historical Foundation; he was a commissioner of the Dutch-American Historical Commission. He also founded The Netherlands Museum (now the Holland Museum) in 1937, where he worked as curator when the war broke out.

To promote the Queen Wilhelmina Fund, Wichers invited Princess Juliana of The Netherlands to Holland in 1941 for the purposes of celebrating the seventy-fifth anniversary of the founding of Hope College. The princess had been living in Canada since the German occupation of The Netherlands. Her husband, German-born Prince Bernhard, joined her for the celebration during leave from military service to England. Their visit did much to remind the people of Holland of their connections to The Netherlands.

Around the time of the royals' visit, The Netherlands saw the need to establish an information center in the United States to promote trade and travel between the two countries, and Wichers spent a great deal of time in Washington,

D.C., and New York helping to develop the service. By 1942, this resulted in the establishment of a Midwest Office of The Netherlands Information Service in Holland, where Wichers worked to develop markets for Dutch goods in the United States and for American enterprises and products in The Netherlands.

As conditions grew worse for people in The Netherlands, Holland discontinued the Tulip Time festival out of respect for their suffering and focused instead on relief work. By the winter of 1944, the Dutch were nearly starving. They were frequently forced to eat tulip bulbs and sugar beets, and they burned furniture and cut trees in order to cook and to heat their homes. In the latter stages of the war, many thousands died of malnutrition.

After the war, in 1946, a four-day Tulip Time festival was renewed, retaining all the pageantry and special features of the previous nine-day events. Tulip bulbs again were available, although in limited quantities because so many had been consumed during the war.

In retrospect, the war had strengthened the ties between Holland and The Netherlands. As a token of thanks to individuals and organizations that provided help, the Dutch sent special colored tiles with the inscription, "Nederland brengt u dankt" (Netherlands brings you thanks). In addition, in 1947 the city of Amsterdam gave Holland a barrel-organ that could be enjoyed by the whole community. It was first paraded down Eighth Street during Tulip Time in 1947 and then for many years afterwards. Considering that Lida Rogers' reading of the English poem "The Barrel-Organ" had inspired the name of the festival back in 1929, the gift was certainly an interesting coincidence.

The 1947 Tulip Time celebrated Holland's centennial, 100 years since its founding by Albertus van Raalte. That year marked the first time a Michigan governor participated in street-scrubbing ceremonies during the parade. Governor Kim Sigler donned a Dutch costume and the photographers had a field day. It became a tradition for future governors as well.

By the start of the 1960s, after almost thirty annual Tulip Time celebrations and the construction of several replica windmills, the idea for an authentic Dutch windmill resurfaced, this time,

*In 1961, local businessman Carter P. Brown, owner of the Castle Park Resort (below), proposed the idea in 1961 of bringing an authentic Dutch windmill to Holland. It is unknown whether he was aware of a similar proposition made in 1929, which was never acted upon.* Joint Archives of Holland.

surprisingly, by a person of English and Scottish roots: Carter Pennell Brown. Brown served as the owner and manager of a popular and long-standing Holland resort, Castle Park, just south of the city.

Ownership of the Lake Michigan waterfront land on which Castle Park stood dated back to the War of 1812 when a soldier acquired it through a land grant. It had changed hands many times before Michael Schwarz, a wealthy businessman, purchased the land. He, his wife, six daughters, and two sons wanted to live away from the mainstream of life. Construction of the multi-storied, medieval-style stone castle began in 1888, and by 1890 the family moved in. However, rural life proved too isolating for them, and the Schwarz family abandoned the castle and moved back to Holland after just two years. The castle stood uninhabited for some time and became a local curiosity and attraction. In 1893, a group of picnickers from Macatawa, led by Dr. John Parr, a minister who was also head of the Chicago Preparatory School, discovered the abandoned building. Intrigued by the castle and acreage, Parr made inquiries and eventually purchased the property to serve as a summertime camp for the boys and girls of his school.

When the camp opened, many of the students' parents were captivated by the natural surroundings and began to purchase property and build summer cottages. After a couple years, Parr and his wife, aware of this mounting interest, closed the camp and converted the castle into a summer hotel. A number of Chicago families, including the Browns from Bloomington, Illinois—Parr's extended family members—summered at what became known as Castle Park.

In 1917, the Parrs retired, and their twenty-three-year-old nephew, Carter Brown, who had been spending his summers at Castle Park since 1905, bought the property in partnership with another Castle Park resident, his new father-in-law, Mr. Wilke, and it grew to have about seventy cottages. After Wilke died in 1924, Brown and his wife continued running Castle Park and developed a strong affinity for the Dutch community of Holland, which led to his suggestion of acquiring a Dutch windmill.

It is unknown whether Carter Brown was aware of the previous proposal of a Dutch windmill in 1929 at the Holland Exchange Club, but he was motivated by the same desire to have a symbol of the Dutch heritage of the community. He brought his proposal to the one person in Holland he thought capable of the task: Willard C. Wichers, then director of the Midwest Office of The Netherlands Information Service. They met over coffee at Wichers' office in August 1961. Brown explained his vision of an authentic working mill along the riverfront east of the River Avenue bridge as the centerpiece of a Dutch park with canals like those in The Netherlands. Klompen dancers could perform in the park during Tulip Time, and both the scale model Klein Nederland" and the barrel-organ donated by the city of Amsterdam could be on permanent display there.

Wichers liked Carter Brown's idea. He immediately realized the historical significance of having an authentic Dutch mill in Holland, and from his work with a number of people in The Netherlands during and after the war he had the proper connections to pursue one. However, he knew that the task would be difficult. The Dutch were on the cusp of signing into law the new Historic Buildings and Ancient Monuments Act, which would forbid the export of windmills.

Two key organizations in The Netherlands held control over the fate of Dutch windmills: Het Ministerie van Onderwijs, Kunsten en Wetenschappen (The Ministry of Education, Arts and Sciences) and Vereniging De Hollandsche Molen (The Dutch Mill Society). The Ministry, founded in 1918 as a division of the Dutch government, began focusing on the condition and status of windmills after World War I, a time when many mills had been destroyed. In 1923, the Minister sent a letter to all of the mayors in The Netherlands pointing out the importance of preserving windmills, and requiring notification whenever demolition of a mill was discussed. The government's action spurred the formation of The Dutch Mill Society that same year. Governed by a board of directors, the society's mission involved preserving, documenting, and restoring windmills, which in some cases meant allowing them to be exported.

However, by the 1960s, the government realized that they were losing their cultural heritage. Of the 9,000 windmills operating in the mid-1800s, only 990 remained, and they had become the leading tourist attraction in The Netherlands. The Ministry and The Dutch Mill Society began to carefully protect them as monuments. If a mill had to be abandoned for the development of highways or other infrastructure, efforts were made to relocate it rather than demolish it. If age or other factors did not permit restoration, the parts would be kept for use in the restoration of other mills. Some mills were converted into homes and others retained as central attractions for new developments.

Initially Wichers did not think obtaining an authentic mill would be possible. Instead he responded to Carter Brown by showing him blueprints for a mill that could be replicated. However, Brown was adamant that it needed to be a mill brought from the old country—one that could continue to operate as a mill, not just a tourist attraction.

Brown was certainly aware of the many historic windmills in various places in the United States, some dilapidated and others opened to tourists as historic sites, but none were operational and all had been built in the United States, some as long ago as 300 years. Immigrants from The Netherlands, England, Germany, Denmark, France and Russia built them in the styles familiar in their homelands.

The first Dutch-style windmill was built in 1625 on Governors Island off the community of New Amsterdam (at the southern tip of today's Manhattan Island) by the Dutch West India Company. It was a post mill, The Netherlands' oldest windmill style, and was used to grind grain to help feed the early colonists. That mill and two others in New Amsterdam played a role in the early economic life of the city that would later become known as New York.

The first English windmill in Ameri-

*One of America's first windmills fabricated by Dutch settlers can be seen to the left of Fort Amsterdam on the southern tip of Manhattan Island, which is today New York City.* Author's Collection.

ca was erected at Flowerdew Hundred in Virginia in 1621. Two years later another English mill was built in Massachusetts between Watertown and Cambridge, but it was moved within the year to a windy hill overlooking the Boston harbor.

The earliest French windmills were built on the river bank west of Fort Pontchartrain (also known as Fort Detroit) beginning in 1707; they had gracefully revolving, fabric-covered blades. French settlers built many more on land that would later be in both Canada and the United States.

The states with the highest concentration of windmills in America were New York, particularly Long Island, and Massachusetts, many on Cape Cod. The flat, windy plains of Illinois provided a region ripe for windmills as well.

Although many of these early windmills had disappeared long ago due to fire, decay, or development, like the two windmills built in Holland in the mid-nineteenth century, some 275 still stood in the United States. Wichers was aware of several windmills considered "Dutch."

A Dutch-syle windmill was built in Lombard, Illinois, in the 1850s by a German craftsman, Louis Blackhaus. The five-story, sixty-eight-foot-tall mill was purchased in 1914 for $8,000 by George and Nelle Fabyan, who moved it about fifteen miles west to their 300-acre country estate, Riverbank, on the Fox River in Batavia. After the deaths of the Fabyans in 1914, the Forest Preserve District of Kane County, Illinois, purchased the estate, and in the 1930s it became the Fabyan Forest Preserve featuring the historic Fabyan Windmill.

Also in Illinois, the Fischer Mill was erected in Elmhurst in 1865 from parts prefabricated in The Netherlands

*The Fabyan Windmill was built in a Dutch style in the 1850s in Illinois to grind grain and was later moved to a private estate. Like the other Dutch-style windmills in the United States, it had fallen into disrepair when Holland began seeking its own mill.* Author's Collection.

to miller Henry Fischer's design and shipped to Illinois. Fischer began grinding by 1867. The mill was later sold, and when wheat farming hit an all-time low in 1894, production at the mill stopped. In 1925, the Mount Emblem Cemetery Association purchased the land and the mill for $10,000, planning to demolish the windmill and other related structures to convert the land into a cemetery. Instead the association decided to preserve the mill as a museum within the cemetery, receiv-

*For years the Fischer Windmill in Elmhurst, Illinois, was considered the oldest in the state, until new research determined it had been built in 1865 rather than 1850.* Illinoiswindmills.org.

*The two Dutch-style windmills in San Francisco, the South 'Murphy' Mill, (top) and the North Mill, (bottom), were built just after the turn of the century in order to pump water in the Golden Gate Park. At the time Holland began seeking its own windmill, these two mills had deteriorated considerably and were no longer operating.* Author's Collection.

mills could pump as much as 40,000 gallons per hour, and operated well into the 1940s when they were replaced by electric pumps. By the 1960s, the windmills had fallen into disrepair.

A windmill in St. Louis, designed in a Dutch and German style, was built in 1916 to serve as a banquet hall and restaurant by the local Anheuser Busch brewing company, a calculated effort to thwart the goals of the Prohibition Movement, and was named after the company's most popular brand of beer, Bevo. It soon became a landmark in the city.

Wichers was certainly familiar with the Farris Mill, an historic attraction at Henry Ford's Greenfield Village in Dearborn, Michigan. One of the country's oldest mills, it had been built in 1633 at Cape Cod by immigrants, styled after those in The Netherlands, although it has more of an English appearance. Its name hails from Captain Samuel Farris, who with the help of others moved the mill to its second location in 1782. Three

*The Bevo Mill in St. Louis, Missouri, was built by Anheuser Busch in 1916 as a restaurant.* Author's Collection.

ing, in 1956, preservation honors from the DuPage County Historical Society.

Two Dutch-style irrigation windmills were erected in the Golden Gate Park in San Francisco, California, by the Park Commission. The Dutch Mill (also called North Mill), a tower-style mill cylindrical in shape, was built in 1903 at a cost of $25,000. Five years later the Murphy Mill, a smock-mill (typically six- or eight-sided sloping upwards resembling a smock or dress), was erected. Both are over ninety feet tall, with wingspans exceeding 100 feet. They sit on stone bases with shingled upper stories. The wind-

*A 1935 newspaper article showed the Farris Windmill as it had stood in West Yarmouth, Massachusetts, since 1633, and (below) the mill after its move in 1935 to Greenfield Village in Michigan.* Author's Collection.

to a reporter, "to their eternal short-sightedness, they saw it as a moss-covered mill in need of repair—a relic that plundering vandals had recently visited—and decided to pass on the offer."

The sale was announced in the press on November 9, 1935, and ignited a torrent of protest against the removal of the Cape's oldest windmill. Six days later, on November 15, a crew from the Ford plant in Somerville, Massachusetts, came and disassembled the mill and put the parts on a truck for transport west to Michigan. Interestingly enough, the departure of the Farris windmill would have a profound effect on Cape Cod. In his book, *The Windmills of New England*, author Daniel Lombardo points out:

*The disappearance of the neglected Farris Windmill was a significant turning point in New England cultural history. Popular writer Joseph Lincoln was galvanized by the loss of the mill. Virtually single-handedly, Lincoln created the twentieth-century image of romantic Old Cape Cod through dozens of books. Lincoln's writing inspired a small industry of windmill miniatures and reproductions on the Cape. Using the Farris Mill as the symbol of the Cape's evaporating history, he called for the preservation of the fabric and image of the Cape. Thanks to Joseph Lincoln and the people he inspired, the loss of the Farris Mill kicked off the Cape's modern preservation movement.*

There had been, according to the *Chicago Tribune*, an authentic, 1860-built Dutch windmill called De Vriendschap (The Friendship), relocated from The Netherlands and erected at the World's Columbian Exposition in Chicago in 1893. Owned by Blooker Cocoa, it was located at the entrance to the wind

generations of the Farris family cared for and operated the mill until 1894, when it was moved to its third location in West Yarmouth, Massachusetts. By then the mill was in poor condition, and its operation was soon discontinued. In the 1930s, when automobile magnate Henry Ford was approaching his eightieth birthday, automobile dealers of Cape Cod presented him with a unique gift—the Farris Windmill—which had recently become available. Its owner, Dr. Edward F. Gleason, first offered to sell the windmill and the land around it to the townspeople of Yarmouth as an historical site, but, according

engine exhibit, and was used to grind cocoa that made treats sold at the fair. The newspaper indicated that millwright A. Verdonk and his sons dismantled and re-erected it specifically for the fair. However, according to the Dutch Mill database, www.molendatabase.org, the most trusted current source for information on all mills erected in The Netherlands, Blooker's Friendship Mill was a replica of the original, which operated in The Netherlands until razed in 1937. It is unknown what happened to the duplicate mill after the fair.

Carter Brown and Willard Wichers were familiar with the authentic mill at the Kellogg estate. The Kelloggs had lived at the manor house until 1942, when in response to World War II, they allowed it to be used as a training camp for the Coast Guard. From 1944 to 1950, the estate was then used as a rehabilitation center for an army hospital. In 1952, after Kellogg's passing, his foundation gave the estate to Michigan State College (University after 1955), allowing for the creation in 1953 of the Kellogg Gull Lake Biological Station of Michigan State College for support of research and teaching. However, the college fo-

*In addition to the replica Dutch cocoa mill on display at the World's Colombian Exposition in Chicago in 1893, windmill manufacturers competed in the most famous marketing displays of modern wind engines, representing the new mills' dominance over the old European designs.* Author's Collection.

cused on its research activities, not promoting its Dutch windmill, which is why few people knew about the mill.

Wichers would not have known anything about another Dutch windmill that had been sent to America. De Veldmuis windmill was built in Zaanstad in North Holland in 1689 as a snuifmolen (tobbaco mill) and changed hands and uses many times. In 1869 it was converted to a sawmill, and by 1916 it had decayed to the point of being unusable. The body was sold to an American and sent to the United States. However, it never arrived. The ship was torpedoed by the Germans and sunk, the same fate as many other non-military ships during World War I.

Willard Wichers knew that the Ministry of Education, Arts and Sciences, created in 1918, which had previously allowed several mills to be exported to America, now had to abide by the new Historic Buildings and Ancient Monuments Act of 1961.

As in America, preservation efforts in The Netherlands began as a private, grass-roots effort that would grow until the point government got involved and wrote laws and set policy. In The Netherlands, Victor de Stuers is considered

*De Veldmuis as it appeared in the early 1900s. It rests in the hull of a shipwreck somewhere on the bottom of the Atlantic Ocean.* J. Vondeling Collection from molendatabase.org.

the founding father of the organized conservation movement. In 1873, at a time when many old buildings were being demolished to make way for industrial progress and development, he wrote a publication called, in translation, *Holland at its Narrowest,* in which he noted the importance of preserving cultural and decorative arts. In 1875, he was appointed as a high official of The Hague (seat of government in The Netherlands), and although there was no official government funding, he started to restore churches, castles, mills, and other historic buildings with the small amounts of money granted him. This work eventually led to the establishment in 1918 of the Ministry of Education, Arts and Sciences and then in 1947 to the establishment of The Netherlands Department of Conservation to maintain the nation's built heritage. The work of these departments then led The Netherlands federal government to sign into law the Historic Buildings and Ancient Monuments Act of 1961, which provided for the legal protection of historic buildings and sites and developed rules to which the own-ers of historic structures must adhere. Among its stipulations, the act prohibitcd the export of windmills and other historic buildings.

Although Wichers probably realized the ramifications of the new act, he and Carter Brown moved forward with the idea of acquiring a Dutch windmill for their city. On October 3, 1961, Brown hosted a meeting in the castle at Castle Park and invited representatives from the Holland City Council, Tulip Time, the Holland Chamber of Commerce, and several other groups. Although those present recognized that the prospect of acquiring a mill could be difficult, Park Superintendent Jacob DeGraaf encouraged the group by pointing out that all of the parks in Holland had been developed on unwanted land and each project had been difficult. The meeting attendees were very enthusiastic about the idea, and First National Bank president Henry S. Maentz invited guests to a lunch meeting the following Tuesday to pursue the idea.

At that meeting on October 10, at the Warm Friend Hotel in downtown

*Willard Wichers had extensive experience dealing with The Netherlands in his position with The Netherlands Information Service and therefore was the perfect person to spearhead Operation Windmill.* Holland Museum Collection.

*Mayor Nelson Bosman stood behind Carter Brown and Willard Wichers' quest to find an authentic Dutch windmill for Holland.* Holland Museum Collection.

*The swampland north of downtown Holland through which the Black River flowed was under consideration as a site for the windmill. The parcels were privately owned but available to the city of Holland.* Holland Sentinel Photograph.

Holland, the group discussed "Operation Windmill," the informal name for the hopeful undertaking. Many notable leaders from the community were invited, including Harry and Fred Nelis, who operated Dutch Village; Lou Hallacy; and Lloyd van Raalte. From among these individuals, Carter Brown soon appointed an executive committee, which included himself, Willard Wichers, Mayor Nelson Bosman, City Manager Herb Holt, First National Bank president Henry Maentz, architects Howard Kameraad and Roger Stroop, Henry Steffens, Roscoe Giles, Jacob DeGraaf, and Jerry Fairbanks. Mayor Bosman, whose approval would most definitely be needed, embraced the idea from the beginning. Fifty-five years old at the time and a 1931 graduate of Hope College, Bosman owned a radio station. He had served on city council since 1957 and had just been elected mayor.

By the following month, the city, with the support of the Holland Township board, opened up the swamplands east of the River Avenue bridge specifically for the dumping of sand, broken cement, stumps, and logs, in hopes of developing suitable solid ground for the park. The *Holland Evening Sentinel* reported on the group's activities, then referred to as "Project Windmill."

On January 19, 1962, an anonymous donor sent the first show of private support: a $1,000 check to the Greater Holland Community Foundation to be used for "Project Windmill." With that, the idea of a park featuring an authentic Dutch windmill took root.

# A Mill for Bill

The city of Holland and the Project Windmill committee moved forward during 1962 with their plans for a windmill and a park in which to showcase it, taking steps to acquire the land and developing sketches for the park. The public continued to show its support. However, Willard Wichers, the man selected to network with the government of The Netherlands because of his connections, had been corresponding with Dutch officials trying to determine the proper people to approach and the procedures for acquiring a mill. The prospects seemed even worse than he first anticipated. In response to his letter offering to travel to The Netherlands to make his case for a mill, Wichers received a reply from Ambassador Jan Herman van Roijen saying, "Don't do it. Save your money and don't come here."

Not one to give up, Wichers kept pushing the idea. During a meeting with van Roijen and his wife, Anna, in Ohio, Anna expressed her personal support. As it turned out, word had reached Ton Koot, a board member of the Dutch Mill Society, who was also in favor of the idea. Wichers realized that he would have to meet in person with the officials in The Netherlands if he hoped to ever get a mill.

*Willard C. Wichers (center) considers the possibility of a windmill for Holland.* Holland Museum Archives.

On Saturday, May 5, 1962, Willard Wichers boarded a KLM Airlines flight to begin negotiations for Project Windmill. From Grand Rapids, he flew to Detroit and then New York, where he boarded a DC-8 for the seven-hour flight to The Netherlands. The plane arrived at 9:40 a.m., and the passengers walked across the tarmac amid a "flurry of picture-taking," as Wichers recorded in his notes. The media was not there to greet *him*, however. Pierre Salinger, press secretary to President John F. Kennedy,

*Willard C. Wichers flew to The Netherlands initially in 1962 to begin negotiations to purchase a windmill.* Holland Museum Archives.

was on the flight. Salinger had scheduled meetings in The Netherlands and West Germany before heading to Moscow to attempt to arrange a face-to-face meeting of Kennedy and Soviet premier Nikita S. Khrushchev to begin peace talks between the United States and the Soviet Union.

Wichers held a significant responsibility. At that point, the Project Windmill committee members and the city of Holland had expended a lot of money and effort to acquire a mill and failure was unthinkable. However, the project could not move forward until Holland received official approval from the Dutch government. Wichers had made arrangements with Dr. David Hofmeijer, commissioner of The Netherlands Immigration Service, with whom he had frequently worked, to escort him through the process of meeting with officials and touring mills. Hofmeijer met Wichers at the Schiphol Airport in Amsterdam and whisked him through customs and to a waiting car. Considering that Wichers did not speak Dutch, he would have had a difficult time without

*Willard Wichers and Dr. David Hofmeijer met in Hofmeijer's office in The Hague.*
Holland Museum Archives.

Hofmeijer's assistance.

"Off we drove through a light rain and the beautiful countryside vivid with blooming tulips and flowering trees, plums, apples and others," Wichers noted of the hour-long drive. "We traveled first to Pinksterbloemplein 76, Dave's address in The Hague," to discuss the windmill project.

Wichers learned that two publications had advertised Holland's desire to purchase a windmill. Hofmeijer himself had inserted an advertisement in *Elsevier's Weekly,* a long-standing and popular Dutch publication. Unbeknownst to Wichers, John Muller, one of the first employees at Parke Davis, a recent immigrant to Holland, and a former Dutch resistance fighter, having heard about Holland's desire to honor its Dutch roots, took it upon himself to place an advertisement in the popular German publication *Der Spiegel.* This notice served to alert the owner of Molen Schrijver in the village of Nijbroek in the Gelderland province, who had already contacted John Muller in Holland.

On behalf of Muller, Wichers, and the city of Holland, Hofmeijer pursued the Molen Schrijver, only to learn that the owner had just sold the mill to two enterprising brothers, Jan de Bruin, eighteen, and Harm de Bruin, twenty, who were now willing to sell the mill to the city of Holland for an incrementally higher price. Neither Hofmeijer nor Wichers wanted to be duped by middlemen, but they considered the mill a remote possibility that should be explored.

On Monday May 7, after an early breakfast, Wichers spent the morning at The Netherlands Immigration Service offices, according to his notes, "busy on the phone and in talks at the office." At noon, he and Hofmeijer had a lunch

*Young would-be entrepreneurs Jan and Harm de Bruin put forth great effort to sell the mill in Nijbroek.* Holland Museum Archives.

meeting with Frederick Stokhuyzen, the president of the Dutch Mill Society, who was a civil engineer and the author of a recently published book on windmills, titled *Molens*. Wichers noted that, "Mr. Stokhuyzen explained how nearly impossible it is now to obtain a mill because laws have been enacted prohibiting anyone from taking down a mill without authority from the provincial and national government." However, he explained, "Ton Koot, who is a member of our board, had made a plea on our behalf and he had in mind that our project might be considered by the authorities in the national monument section of the Ministry of Education, together with a request from the authorities in Curaçao."

*Willard Wichers met with Frederick Stokhuyzen, president of the Dutch Mill Society, and an author of several books on windmills.* Holland Museum Archives.

Wichers learned that Curaçao wanted an authentic mill after learning that the neighboring island of Aruba, one of three islands that made up The Netherlands Antilles north of the Venezuelan coast, had gotten one. Developers of the recently built Condada Caribbean Hotel, a luxury beach-front hotel on Aruba, had been granted permission for a Dutch mill as part of an aggressive marketing plan to attract more tourists. The windmill would house a restaurant called "De Olde Molen." Aruba had been allowed to purchase the grain mill, Molen van Jonker, that had been standing idle in Wedderveer, Gronigen, since a storm damaged it in 1929.

Wichers understood that The Netherlands government had authorized the mill for Aruba because The Netherlands Antilles was part of the Kingdom of The Netherlands. To make their case for a mill being exported to America, Hofmeijer and Wichers spoke at great length with Stokhuyzen about the Dutch settlers who founded Holland, showing him aerial photos and maps of the river area they were considering as a potential site. Stokhuyzen suggested that although he could make no definite promises, he felt that the Holland project happened to be very well timed following the Aruba approval and the request from Curaçao. He expressed doubt that it could ever be undertaken in the future. After that meeting, Wichers recorded in his notes that "if we can obtain the Ministry of Education's approval, we can be assured that Mr. Stokhuyzen would cooperate also."

Next, Hofmeijer and Wichers traveled to Amsterdam to meet with Arie J. de Koning, the technical advisor to the Dutch Mill Society. Wichers described him as "an architect who devotes most of his time to the preservation and restoration of windmills, although he does conduct some private architectural work. He maintains a complete card index on mills in the Netherlands."

De Koning was born in Wognum in the province of North Holland and received an engineering degree in 1946 and an architectural degree in 1950. He and a partner ran an architectural firm in Amsterdam and had designed numerous homes for senior citizens as well as schools and factories. De Koning became interested in windmills during the war when many were put back into service to compensate for the lack of electricity. In fact, he had helped restore a mill in his own home town. After the war, he began consulting for the Dutch Mill Society and became the organization's technical advisor. He had since supervised the restoration of hundreds of historic mills in The Netherlands, including the one in the famous Keukenhof Gardens in Lisse, one of the world's largest flower gardens.

Wichers specifically inquired about the mill in Nijbroek that the de Bruin brothers were now offering for sale. Checking his notes, de Koning advised against considering that mill. It had been built in 1605, he explained, and its body was in poor condition due to dry rot and extreme age. At the meeting, Wichers noted, "We talked at some length about the construction of mills and Mr. de Koning felt our best bet lies in the Groningen province providing that we can obtain necessary authority."

De Koning recommended a grain mill, which would typically be in better condition than a water-pumping mill or sawmill and which would serve a useful role in America. He estimated that such a mill would cost between 1,000 and 3,000 guilders. He proposed setting the mill atop a new-built brick base (a style called stellingmolen) that would be in keeping with the traditional Dutch windmill design seen in many grain mills. The bricks would have to be new, but could be manufactured similar to typical period bricks in The Netherlands. "Because of the problems encountered in covering it with the more traditional reed thatching [like the mill in Nijbroek]," Wichers noted, "[de Koning] proposed oak shingles."

After the meeting with de Koning,

*Lengthy discussions with government officials in The Netherlands and the Dutch Mill Society finally resulted in permission for the city of Holland to purchase a windmill. Pictured left to right are Frederick Stokhuyzen, F.P.Th. Rohling, Willard Wichers, and Dr. David Hofmeijer.* City of Holland, Windmill Island Archives.

Hofmeijer recommended that Wichers invite him to Holland in the very near future to look over the site and make specific suggestions. Next, the pair headed over to the Schiller Hotel, which, according to Hofmeijer, was "the favorite meeting place for journalists and artists." Arrangements had been made for Wichers to meet with Friso Endt, a journalist with the Amsterdam newspaper *Het Parool* that had its roots as a resistance paper during the war; he also served as a correspondent for *Time-Life* magazine. The intent of the interview was to garner public support to allow a mill to be sent to Holland, Michigan. Within days, Endt's article appeared in *Het Parool* under a clever headline that the committee would adopt as an unofficial slogan for the windmill project: "Een Molen voor Bill" (A Mill for Bill). That article, and the many more that it spawned, would generate countrywide attention for the project.

On Tuesday morning, May 8, Hofmeijer and Wichers headed off to visit several mills. On their way, they stopped in Appledoorn in the Gelderland province in the center of The Netherlands, where Wichers' grandfather was born. Appledoorn was only a few miles southwest of Nijbroek, so they decided to tour that mill. Wichers immediately recognized that the mill was, indeed, in very poor condition, just as de Koning had indicated; it had been moved generations ago from Zaandam where it had served as a waterpumping mill. Wichers was definitely not interested in that mill for Holland.

They next traveled to meet with a W. Breunis, who had an interest in a mill at Nieuwleusen in the Overijssel province that he would allow to be taken down for 3,000 guilders. After inspecting the mill, they learned that Breunis did not have government permission to demolish it, so they checked another mill off their list.

*The Molen Schrijver in Nijbroek was eventually granted a demolition permit in 1963 when no buyers could be found.* D. Zweers Collection from molendtatbase.org.

After lunch, the windmill hunters traveled to Zuidlaren in Drenthe, where Hofmeijer introduced Wichers to forty-one-year-old Jan Diederick "Diek" Medendorp, a millwright descended from a long line of millwrights and millers in The Netherlands. After graduating from technical college in 1946 and later a miller school, one of his first projects was to restore De Wachter (The Watchman), a Zuidlaren mill built in 1851 that his own grandfather had purchased and operated in 1895. Medendorp soon became the premier expert on building and restoring windmills. With de Koning, he worked on what would be one of The Netherlands' most visible mill restorations at the new Keukenhof Gardens, an eighty-acre park southwest of Amsterdam with seven million tulips. The Holland American Line donated the funds to acquire the parts from several mills to be reassembled into a hybrid windmill by Medendorp; one was the Molen Bergeman, a grain mill originally built in 1862 at Meedhuizen in Groningen. In fact, during that project, de Koning introduced Medendorp to a neighbor of his, who would later become his wife. The two men had been working closely together ever since.

Hofmeijer and Wichers spent the following day in "mill country," in the northern Netherlands, seeing mills in Groningen where de Koning thought the best prospects lay. They toured mills at Loppersum, Winsum, Garnwerd, Feerwerd, and Fransum, and went on to Kollum to see the mill owned by a Mr. Visser, who offered to sell if he could get a permit to take it down. (Interestingly, Visser never got the permit, and the mill mysteriously burned later that year.)

Wichers also made a stop at "Dalfsen in Overijssel to confer with Mr. Kloosterman of the weekly magazine *De Molenaar* (The Miller)" about whether he knew of any available mills.

On Thursday morning, May 10, Wichers took the train to Amsterdam to meet with Ton Koot of the Dutch Mill Society, who worked as general secretary at the Rijksmuseum. Koot provided a tour of the famous museum and the two discussed the project at length. Wichers kept such a busy schedule during his trip that he relied on his notes in order to report his progress to the windmill committee in Holland. He signed his letter, "With affectionate wishes from a Dutchman with windmills in his head."

While Wichers concluded his trip with positive feelings about the probability of being allowed a mill, he knew that the Dutch authorities would not allow the export of a mill unless they determined that Holland had an appropriate site and the funds for its development.

Following Wichers' trip, the Holland City Council invited Arie de Koning of the Dutch Mill Society to Holland as Hofmeijer had suggested. That would prove to be a critical step in eventually receiving permission for a mill.

*Carter Brown, left, initially conceived the idea of bringing a Dutch windmill to Holland. Henry S. Maentz, Willard C. Wichers, and Mayor Nelson Bosman served with him as early leaders in Project Windmill.* City of Holland, Windmill Island Archives.

De Koning arrived at the Detroit airport on July 13, 1962, for a two-week stay. Committee members met him there, and the next day the group toured the Ford assembly plant at River Rouge and Greenfield Village, where they saw the Farris Windmill that had originally hailed from Cape Cod, Massachusetts.

In Holland, de Koning's objective was to determine if the city possessed a suitable site for a mill, which the committee stressed must not be *just* a showpiece, but a working mill. Consequently, he sought to identify a location that included access to wind with consideration of direction, speed, and velocity. The ideal site called for a sweep of flat lowlands with no trees, buildings, or other obstructions. The committee proposed several places, including the properties northeast of the northside bridge, the city dump, the lake frontage between Kollen Park and H. J. Heinz Company, and the location they believed to be the most suitable: the two properties owned by the Kempker and Hyma families on the south side of the Black River between the River Avenue bridge and the C&O Railroad bridge. De Koning toured

*(Above left to right) Carter Brown, Dutch Mill Society technical advisor Arie J. de Koning, and Holland Park superintendent Jacob DeGraaf helped scout possible sites for a windmill on foot (above) and in a boat (right).* City of Holland, Windmill Island Archives.

these sites on foot and then the committee arranged an aerial reconnaissance. That flight resulted in de Koning's determining that the Kempker and Hyma properties would indeed be the most appropriate spots. The committee erected a yellow flag at the preferred spot on the Hyma property, but de Koning recommended that both parcels be acquired for the project. Interestingly, the chosen spot was just a half mile directly east of the very first windmill erected in Holland in 1848. The newly settled Dutch immigrants who built that mill had the same instinct for a suitable location as de Koning did more than a century later.

The community showed its support for the project and bid de Koning goodbye at a barbecue sponsored by the Jaycees at which he was the honored guest. Over one thousand residents attended.

Upon de Koning's approval of the site, Project Windmill moved forward more quickly. The city council exercised a lease option agreement with John Kempker and his wife for the 128 acres of lowland property, calling for a $500 option for two years, a ten-year rental period at $3,000 per year, and then a purchase price of $42,000. The city planned to acquire the thirty-acre Hyma property on similar terms.

Because the council chose not to use any tax revenues for the project, it decided to pursue a federal 50/50 matching grant under the Public Facilities Acceleration Act of 1962 for the funds to purchase, ship, and re-erect the mill as well as to develop the island. The city also retained the services of local architects Kaameraad and Stroop and the law firm Wright, McKean and Cudlip as bond attorneys to proceed with the preparation of a revenue bond ordinance to cover the city's portion of the funding. The entire project was estimated at $900,000, but within a few weeks, the city decided to split it into phases and pursue $450,000 to cover the windmill, the gardens, and the infrastructure for what was then being referred to as Windmill Island, postponing the development of a golf course and other structures to phase two.

In October, the city hired Dr. Frank

*Local architects Kaameraad and Stroop developed plans and renderings based on Arie de Koning's recommendations.* City of Holland, Windmill Island Archives.

W. Suggitt of Michigan State University, a consultant on tourism, to prepare a study of the potential revenues of Windmill Island. At that time tourism in Michigan was a $2.6 million industry, an amount expected to increase due to the growth of income, leisure, recreation, and travel. Suggitt's study indicated that Holland could expect 500,000 visitors during its second full season and that the number would increase by 5 to 10 percent each year thereafter. At one dollar per adult for admission, he felt the island would be self-sustaining. He also estimated that souvenir and concessions sales could bring in an additional dollar per person. Suggitt recommended pursuing $800,000 to fully develop the property immediately, which, he felt, could quickly be repaid through ticket sales.

In November the city council learned the project would not be eligible for the federal grant unless all the work could be done through a competitive bid. Since the committee had not even been offered a single mill, it knew that buying a mill competitively would be impossible. The city would have to pursue funding elsewhere.

In early December 1962, Dr. David Hofmeijer of The Netherlands Immigration Service made a visit to Holland. The fact that he interrupted a personal around-the-world trip to do so boded well for the project. He met with Wichers, with whom he had spent so much time in The Netherlands, and the Project Windmill committee and toured the chosen site. He provided a hopeful update on the progress of the talks in The Netherlands.

By that time, Aruba had already received the Molen van Jonker, a stelling-molen-style grain mill, and millwright Diek Medendorp, whom Wichers met in The Netherlands, was in the process of re-erecting it on the island and converting it to a restaurant.

Finally, on January 30, 1963, Willard Wichers received one of the most important correspondences of the project. The letter from Frederick Stokhuyzen, the president of the Dutch Mill Society, said in part,

*We can tell you that the Ministry of Education, Arts and Science of our Government has given her approval and cooperation for exporting a Dutch mill from here to Holland, Michigan, for this purpose.*

*You can see this as an exception to the existing regulation thanks to the sympathetic relations between our mutual*

*Molen de Jonker as it appeared in The Netherlands (top) and after its relocation to Aruba where it became known as De Olde Molen.* molendatabase.org and City of Holland, Windmill Island Archives.

*governments as well as between your and our people, especially between you and your committee and our Society.*

*Without any doubt we may say that this will be the only mill that will be expedited from here to America and we hope that you'll feel happy in the idea that you'll possess then the only original Dutch windmill in the United States.*

*We will do our utmost to provide you a good original mill for the purpose and we are convinced that we can help you with a good specimen in due time.*

In that same letter, Stokhuyzen pointed out that Diek Medendorp had been given a demolition permit for the relatively small poldermolen De Kooi from Kantens, Groningen, and now had the disassembled parts in his possession and was prepared to fabricate any additional components needed to make it operational. Wichers knew, though, that the committee wished to publicize the dismantling of a mill as part of the marketing effort, and that a small hybrid mill would not be acceptable. In fact, af-

*De Kooi windmill in Kantens, Groningen, as it existed in disrepair in 1960, just before Diek Medendorp disassembled it.* Bert Lanjouw collection from molendatabase.org.

ter Wichers forwarded the letter to City Manager Herbert Holt, Holt quickly replied: "Because of the magnitude and importance that Project Windmill has achieved, not only locally, but nationally and perhaps internationally, it seems to us most important that we get the best possible mill available from all points of view." Holt further stipulated that "the mill shall have existed as a unit as well as being structurally and mechanically sound."

Now that permission had been granted, the committee's expectations became more particular. The members had agreed that they wanted to acquire a grain mill directly from a Dutch miller and promote the mill's former history in The Netherlands as a foundation for what would be its new history in Holland. In fact, they wanted to make a film that would publicize the mill—capturing footage of it in place in The Netherlands, the disassembly, the transportation across the ocean, reassembly, and the dedication in Holland—to reflect the great importance of the undertaking.

A little over a week later, Wichers received another letter from The Netherlands, this one from F. P. Th. Rohling, the director of the Department of Archeology and Protection of Nature within the Ministry of Education, Arts and Sciences. Rohling heralded the significance of the approval, but overlooked the Dutch windmill that had previously been sent to the Kellogg estate several decades earlier. In part Rohling wrote,

*It certainly constitutes a very great exception that with the approval of the Ministry of Education, Arts and Science a Dutch windmill is exported. On the contrary, The Netherlands Government is constantly doing its utmost to restore*

*the mills and to keep them in good order, as they undoubtedly are a very typical feature of the Dutch landscape.*

*So, if my department consented in the export of two windmills—one to [Aruba], and one to Holland, Michigan, the only reason for this attitude is to be found in the historical ties between these cities and The Netherlands. As regards the mill for Holland, Michigan—very likely the last mill which will be sent to America—we thought that of all places in the United States, your dear city, bearing the name of good old Holland, ought to have the privilege of having the only original Dutch windmill in the States.*

With the blessing of both organizations, the search continued for a mill that fit the criteria of the city of Holland. Although Arie de Koning and Wichers had long ago ruled out the mill in Nijbroek, its owners, the de Bruin brothers, had spent considerable effort promoting the mill and had succeeded in getting some media attention in The Netherlands and the United States. The Atlanta, Georgia, *Journal* reported how the brothers had been trying to hawk their mill to such places as Disneyland, among others. Holland's city manager Herb Holt expressed his distaste about their marketeering efforts in a letter to Willard Wichers on January 31, 1963:

*We feel that if the imported, original Dutch windmill concept is to be exploited for private commercial gain, in the long run it can only cheapen the historical and cultural value of such an undertaking. If a ... Dutch windmill ... is to become just another display item in the wonder-world of Disneyland, the whole idea loses not only its significance but much of its status and certainly its*

*uniqueness ... If there exists certain discarded and abandoned mills, they should be provided an appropriate retirement and not placed on the auction block for outside commercial exploitation.*

David Hofmeijer of The Netherlands Immigration Service had stayed on top of that issue since it first came to his attention the previous May. He shared what he knew of the de Bruin brothers with Wichers and the windmill committee in a March 1963 letter: "The family of de Bruin did a very bad deal in buying the old mill we saw at Nijbroek. They are more or less in a panic. Their purchase of the mill in May 1962 for 10,000 guilders required they demolish it within a year. They recently learned that it would cost another 7,000 guilders to have it torn down."

Hofmeijer had little sympathy for the situation, since it was clear the family was attempting to make money by offering a decrepit mill to the Americans at a steep cost. "I think they should accept their loss now and not try to have all sorts of articles in magazines," he wrote.

Hofmeijer concluded his correspondence by noting that Aric de Koning had informed him of a possible mill in the province of Friesland. "So we keep our fingers crossed," he wrote. However, it became clear that the Ministry of Education, Arts, and Sciences expected Holland to have the money in place for the entire project before it released a windmill. Consequently, the committee spent the balance of 1963 working to secure the funding of $450,000 for phase one. By April, James Pollock, a bond consultant from Kalamazoo, started working with the committee to develop plans to market revenue bonds for the project.

Meanwhile, Kammeraad and Stroop began preparing plans for Windmill Island, which included the mill, large beds of flowers, a miller's house, a barn, a canal and dike around the island, parking, roads, and a gate house. As inspiration, Wichers made specific inquiry into the two early 1900-built Dutch windmills in San Francisco by contacting the manager at the Golden Gate Park. Members of the committee also traveled to Batavia, Illinois, on August 28, 1963, to tour the 1850s-built Fabyan Mill in the Fabyan Forest Preserve. All three mills, they learned, had fallen into disrepair and were badly in need of restoration.

As the project came closer to reality, there was much debate between the members of the city council and private citizens over whether the island would be open on Sundays. The council tabled this controversial decision until nearer the opening.

By October, the council approved an ordinance calling for $450,000 in revenue bonds to be paid off in twenty years, setting the sale for March 18, 1964. "If the bonds are sold," City Manager Herb Holt wrote to Carter Brown, "then the fat is in the fire from that point on."

Five months later and fifteen months after The Netherlands government had agreed to export a mill to Holland, the *Holland Evening Sentinel* made a sizzling announcement: "Project Windmill Bond Issue Sold—Completion Date Set for 1965." Goodbody and Company of New York had offered an interest rate of 4.224 percent, the lower of two bids. With funds in hand, the committee wasted no time in beginning a search for a manager for Windmill Island, and Willard Wichers wasted no time informing Stokhuyzen and his other contacts in The Netherlands that Holland had the money in hand, pointing out that per the terms of the bond sale, the windmill must be operational

by May 1965 to draw the Tulip Time crowds.

Stokhuyzen responded on April 2, noting that Holland would have to move quickly in order to meet that deadline. He again offered De Kooi mill that Medendorp had already disassembled. It could be shipped immediately. But he also let Wichers know that the Dutch Mill Society was in negotiations over a grain mill from the village of Vinkel, North Brabant. Although it was in bad shape, it was still standing and significantly larger than De Kooi. Medendorp would be available to take that mill apart as well. "If it turns out that we can't acquire this mill..." he cautioned Wichers, "... you can't wait any longer for one of big size and 'history.'"

Wichers talked to the committee and responded to Stokhuyzen a week later noting Holland's preference for the Vinkel mill based on the fact that it was larger and still standing. He indicated he would come in June to purchase the mill if the Dutch Mill Society's negotiations proved successful.

The committee was ready to purchase the mill in Vinkel, but at that point Wichers had not been given any specifics about it. He must have asked David Hofmeijer to investigate the history of the mill, because more than a month later, and just two weeks before Wichers planned to leave for The Netherlands, Hofmeijer provided a detailed history prepared by J.G.W. Swagers. The mill's name was De Zwaan, meaning The Swan.

Many windmills in The Netherlands had been named De Zwaan, but this particular De Zwaan was a korenmolen (grain mill) located in the southern portion of The Netherlands in the rural village of Vinkel, North Brabant, in the municipality of Nuland. (Incidentally,

just ten miles north of St. Oedenrode where historians believe The Netherlands' first windmill was built to grind grain in 1299). According to Swagers, who got his information from the current mill owner and municipal officials, miller H. F. de Vocht of Helmond (about twenty-five kilometers south of Vinkel) purchased a used smock mill-style body from the province of North Holland and erected it in 1884 as a grondmolen (mill on level ground), where it operated with

*Piet Van Schaijk (left) and his son Willem van Schayk owned De Zwaan successively when it was in Vinkel.* Courtesy of Stichting de Vinkelse Molen.

"blue stones" to grind grain. (Later research uncovered that Henricus Franciscus de Vocht, who was born in 1835, had for years operated the grain mill Molen van De Vocht in Helmond before erecting De Zwaan in Vinkel. Four months after his daughter Petronella Maria married Petrus (Piet) van Schaijk in July 1886, his son-in-law Piet took over operation of De Zwaan.)

Because of a newly constructed church in 1900, De Zwaan was deprived of the westerly winds, and so in 1902 van Schaijk hired an Evert Michels to move it hundreds of yards away to a small mound of land, where it became a bergmolen (mill on a mound). During the move that took six weeks, the wooden blades were replaced with steel blades made by Gebroeders Pot. (A later story surfaced that indicated van Schaijk was so mad at the church for blocking his wind that he did not attend services for six weeks.) Then in 1908, the blue

*The only photograph of De Zwaan on Dennenlaan in Vinkel where it stood for sixteen years until a new church interfered with its airspace, leading to its move to Lindenlaan, a short distance away. Note that the mill originally stood on flat ground.* Courtesy of Stichting de Vinkelse Molen.

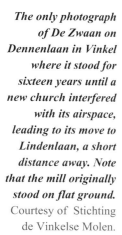

*De Zwaan stood at Vinkel in North Brabant since 1884. According to the authorities in The Netherlands, De Zwaan was built in Krommenie, northwest of Amsterdam, in 1761, although little information beyond that was provided.*

Groningen

Friesland

Drenthe

IJsselmeer

North Holland

Flevo-

-land

Overijssel

Krommenie

Amsterdam

Gelderland

South Holland

Utrecht

Vinkel

North Brabant

Zeeland

Limburg

GERMANY

BELGIUM

stones were replaced with self-sharpening artificial stones. The original blue stones would be available to move with De Zwaan to Holland.

Piet and Petronella van Schaijk's son Willem van Schayk (name spelling changed by then), who was born in 1887, eventually took over the mill.

Damage during the war rendered the blades inoperable. Van Schayk tried to raise funds to restore the mill, but the local municipalities would not support him, and so the mill had become available for Holland.

Swagers also noted that the burgemeester (mayor) of Nuland had planned some festivities to greet Wichers in Vinkel and celebrate the sale of the mill. The mayor also expressed his own interest, as well as that of Willem van Schayk, to travel to Holland to participate in celebrations after the mill had been moved.

Because Wichers had only been given information about the mill after it was moved to Vinkel, he looked forward to learning more about its history before 1884 when it was in North Holland.

Arie de Koning scheduled a meeting between all the participants for June 8 in Vinkel. Wichers would need to be there to finalize all the arrangements. As Wichers prepared for his upcoming trip, in April the Holland City Council retained the services of fifty-two-year-old Jerry Fairbanks, a former Holland resident, as a part-time director of Windmill Island. Fairbanks had attended public school and Hope College in Holland and graduated from Michigan State College in 1934 with a bachelor of science degree as a landscape architect. He previously had supervised the state park system in West Virginia and, after serving in the military, worked for the Huron-Clinton Metropolitan Authority doing master planning and development of Kensington Park. Currently the owner and general manager of the Au Sable Ranch and Ski Club, Fairbanks would spend two days every other week in Holland overseeing the details of the project's development. After Windmill Island opened the following year, the city council would determine if Fairbanks would stay on as manager.

One of the first things he managed was the construction by the L. W. Lamb Company of a temporary bridge to the island so that materials and equipment could reach the site. Soon thereafter, soil borings taken on the Hyma property at the spot intended for the windmill raised concerns over that piece of ground, and the team quickly adjusted its plans to position the mill farther east to a more solid piece of land on the Kempker property. Wichers packed the new plans and other technical data to take with him to The Netherlands for de Koning's approval.

By June 1964, only eleven months remained before Windmill Island was scheduled to open at Tulip Time in 1965. Per the terms of the bond issue, Windmill Island had to be generating income

*Jerry Fairbanks, a landscape architect, then owner-manager of a winter sports center in Northern Michigan, was hired as the manager for Windmill Island to help see the project through to completion and beyond.* City of Holland, Windmill Island Archives.

by then, so time was of the essence. The needs were many: final construction plans from the architects; bidding out the work by the city council; roads, parking lot, bridges, buildings, and mill base built by the selected contractors; garden plans developed by a landscape designer; and thousands of tulip bulbs planted by gardeners. Of the utmost importance, though, was that Diek Medendorp had to be ready to disassemble, ship, and reassemble the mill. Only one thing stood in the way of the project: The Dutch government required a six-month waiting period before it would export the mill, leaving too little time to complete the work in Holland. After overcoming so many obstacles, Wichers faced a last hurdle: a waiver of the waiting period.

On June 6, 1964, Wichers boarded a plane for The Netherlands, armed with official documentation as agent for the city of Holland to acquire De Zwaan, negotiate the waiver, participate in local festivities celebrating the sale, and oversee the dismantling and filming of the mill.

Wichers arrived at Schiphol Airport in Amsterdam to even more excitement this time. "The Beatles were about to leave, so it was quite a sight," he wrote in his report, "but those thousands of teenagers weren't looking for MILL BILL."

At the airport, Wichers participated in a press conference. Reporters questioned which mill he would buy. Wichers responded, "Gentlemen, until I have the opportunity to confer with the officers of De Hollandsche Molen, I can't say which mill is to be given our first consideration." When pushed he said, "The mill of Vinkel is under consideration."

That evening Wichers learned "some pretty grim facts from Arie de Koning and David Hofmeijer," according to his notes. Apparently in the two years since a mill

for Holland was approved, several more mills had been destroyed, and sentiment on the board of the Dutch Mill Society had changed. At that moment, Wichers did not know if the society would follow through and allow a purchase.

The news hit Wichers hard; that night he became quite ill, and had to be immediately hospitalized in The Hague. "The psychological shock was so great that it may have made me ripe for this illness," he wrote home, avoiding the private nature of his bladder infection.

Not about to give up, Wichers set up a command post in the hospital while doctors treated him, and he carried on with the many steps needed to consummate the purchase of a mill.

On Monday, June 8, 1964, Wichers roused from his hospital bed and, along with Dr. David Hofmeijer and Frederick Stokhuyzen, traveled to Vinkel where they met Arie de Koning, Diek Medendorp, and other officials to proceed with discussions over the sale of the mill De Zwaan. Vinkel impressed Wichers as a small village of another time. Its jurisdiction was divided between five neighboring municipalities and because the mill was located in the segment belonging to Nuland, the Nuland mayor became involved as well.

Willard Wichers was immediately impressed with the large size of the mill—it had a wingspan of 25.5 meters (about eighty feet). Only then did he learn more about the early history of the mill. De Zwaan, de Koning explained, had been built in 1761 in Krommenie, in the Zaan District in the North Holland province, just a few miles northwest of Amsterdam. It had been crafted as a hennepklomper (hemp mill) to replace the original De Zwaan, an oliemolen (oil mill) built in 1649. That mill was destroyed by fire

*A view of De Zwaan in Vinkel a few years before its move to Holland.* Holland Museum Archives.

milling had been a continuous way of life for the van Schayk family. The onset of war in 1939 had changed all that.

North Brabant saw extensive combat activity during the time of the German occupation, particularly during Operation Market Garden in September 1944, the largest airborne battle in history. Under Field Marshal Bernard Montgomery, the Allies sent thousands of aircraft and armored vehicles and hundreds of thousands of troops to push north through The Netherlands into the Ruhr Valley and attempt to move into Germany. The operation was the only major Allied defeat of the Northwest European campaign, and unfortunately left destruction in its path.

During the early time of the German occupation, the Ministry of Education, Arts and Sciences tallied 1,467 working windmills still in existence, and another 483 that stood in various states of decay. An inventory made after the war showed only 1,306 working mills and 473 that had been partially destroyed, a loss of fully 171 mills. In that time, De Zwaan had been reduced from a working mill, last operated in 1940, to one that could now only function with a Diesel motor. Van Schayk did his best to maintain the windmill, patching the holes and covering the body of the mill with asphalt paper, but it needed costly repairs and restoration to be operational again—money that Van Schayk did not have.

As De Zwaan decayed further, so did other Dutch mills. Another inventory done in 1960 indicated that only 991 windmills still existed The Netherlands. Van Schayk had been unable to secure the funding required for the restoration in the two decades following the war, and so it came to be that Arie de Koning negotiated De Zwaan's availability for Holland.

in 1761. In its original location it sat on a base as a stellingmolen, coincidentally just as de Koning had planned for Holland. When steam power began replacing wind in metropolitan areas in the 1880s, De Zwaan, like many windmills, was sold off to a more rural community. That is how it came to be in Vinkel.

Wichers was thrilled when he heard the news; not only was De Zwaan over two hundred years old, but it would be restored to its original configuration as a stellingmolen, adding greatly to the mill's significance as a heritage site and attraction.

Since its relocation, De Zwaan had become a beloved edifice in Vinkel and

Wichers made an inspection climb of the mill with Diek Medendorp, the millwright assigned by the Dutch Mill Society to dismantle, restore, and reassemble the mill. Medendorp certainly had the necessary qualifications, and he also spoke some English, an important skill considering how closely he would have to work with contractors in Holland.

Although the mill sat on a mound, Wichers learned that the mound had been excavated and a brick foundation had been built to form a lower level, divided into several rooms where the miller stored the grain and flour. American barns often borrowed this design, siting barns on a small hill. Horses could enter their stalls on the lower level, while the main barn could be accessed on the upper level.

During that tour, Wichers was introduced to Jan H.H. Adriaens, identified as the present owner of the mill. He was a millwright from the firm Gebroeders Adriaens (Adriaens Brothers) from Weert in the Limberg province just southeast of Vinkel. The firm had been in business since before the turn of the century but struggled during the war years when it was difficult for millwrights to make a living. The passage of the Historic Buildings and Ancient Monuments Act of 1961 provided many new opportunities for the firm as well as for other millwrights.

Wichers was disturbed when he learned that a millwright owned the mill; he was under the impression that Holland would be purchasing the mill directly from van Schayk, the mill's third-generation owner. When he raised concerns about a brokered sale, Stokhuyzen and de Koning made it quite clear that it would be many months before they could locate a mill that would meet all the criteria of Holland, Michigan, essentially indicating that it was De Zwaan or nothing.

*De Zwaan as it appeared as a bergmolen (mound mill) in Vinkel just before its move to Holland, Michigan.* Courtesy of Stichting de Vinkelse Molen.

Adriaens pointed out that a number of the timbers in the mill were Northern European pine typical of Scandinavia and were quite sound, while others would have to be replaced. The cap, which is vital to the operation, appeared solid as well as most of the machinery, the blades, the huge axle, and the drive post.

Contrary to de Koning's description of the mill's history, Adriaens indicated that its origins were not totally clear—it could have been an industrial mill, or perhaps a sawmill. No photographs of the mill as it existed in Krommenie had been located, but he had also concluded that it originally sat on a base to capture the upper air currents.

*This rare photograph of De Zwaan shows the mill during its working life when it was still powered by wind in Vinkel before World War II. Note the church in the background, which prompted the mill's move to this alternate location on Lindenlaan in 1902. It was erected as a mound mill here to capture more wind.*
Courtesy of Stichting de Vinkelse Molen.

Following Wichers' inspection, he, Frederick Stokhuyzen, David Hofmeijer, Diek Medendorp, and Jan Adriaens met with the Nuland burgermeester, G.A.J. van Heereveld, in his office. Wichers described the mayor as "a colorful Brabanter," noting that "it is the first time I ever encountered a business official smoking a long, clay Gouda pipe. He is not a large man and to see him behind his large desk with the clay pipe was delightful."

The objective of that meeting was to acquire title to the mill and then work with the provincial and municipal authorities for permission to dismantle and ship everything immediately. The owner, Adriaens, was invited to state his firm's terms. In a move perhaps designed to increase the mill's value, Adriaens quickly pointed out that in the short time since his firm had acquired the mill from van Schayk, the people of Vinkel had been pressuring him to keep the mill and restore it on site for the community. According to him, two of the most vocal local leaders, the bishop and the school headmaster, were solidly opposed to the sale. However, Adriaens acknowledged that he had made a pledge to Arie de Koning, and he assured those present at the meeting that he would fulfill that commitment. He asked a sum of 10,000 guilders, which was significantly higher than the going rate previously described to Wichers.

After some haggling, Adriaens agreed to sell the mill for 8,000 guilders (approximately $2,800, which represents about $21,000 at the time of this book's publishing). Before concluding the deal, the mayor contacted officials at the Ministry of Education and the province of North Brabant by telephone. After receiving their approvals, Adriaens and Wichers executed the papers, which were signed by all the parties as well.

Most important, the provincial authorities waived the normal six-month waiting period.

Only then did the mayor tell Wichers and the others present that he had been forced to cancel the planned festivities due to negative local feelings about losing the mill. Indeed, a Dutch newspaper article titled, "Verdriet in Vinkel, 'De Zwaan' verdwijnt," (Sadness in Vinkel, 'De Zwaan' disappears) noted that,

*Festivities are cancelled that had been planned for Saturday to celebrate that the mill "The Swan" will be moved from Vinkel to the city of Holland in the American state of Michigan. The people of Vinkel have objections to a festive celebration occasioned by the loss of a splendid mill. The inhabitants of Vinkel consider this removal of their fondly cherished more as a funeral ceremony. As they see it, a festive mood does not fit this occasion.*

The mood in Vinkel following the sale was much like the mood in Cape Cod when the Farris Mill was taken down to ship to Henry Ford's Greenfield Village in 1935, and in stark contrast to the feelings in Holland. Members of the windmill committee were thrilled when Wichers sent a cablegram announcing the purchase of the mill. Although he explained in a follow-up letter that, "it appears quite certain now that our mill has a long history and is quite old, perhaps dating back to the beginning of the 18th century," he also recognized that he had not been given anything in writing confirming its lineage before relocation to Vinkel. "We will have to continue researching this history," he concluded.

In fact, nearly a half century would pass before De Zwaan's actual provenance would come to light.

# Flight of the Swan

When the people in the North Brabant Province learned that De Zwaan would be immediately dismantled and shipped to a city called Holland in the United States, they were unquestionably saddened. Although the mill had been the private property of Willem van Schayk, it had become such a landmark—like other windmills in The Netherlands—that the community felt a sense of ownership. For many, losing the mill was like losing an old friend. When the news of the mill's sale was broadcast over the radio, a very sick young teen, Nico Jurgens, who had a tremendous love for windmills, begged his father to take him from his sick bed to see the mill before it disappeared across the ocean. To appease Nico, his father made the forty-five-kilometer drive from the west side of Eindhoven to the small town of Vinkel so that the boy could get a parting glimpse of De Zwaan while it was still standing. Nico brought along his camera and captured the mill on film so that he could always remember it. His love for windmills and the loss of De Zwaan made such an impression on Nico that as an adult he became one of The Netherlands' most respected mill scholars and a mill restoration consultant.

*(Opposite) Among the last images captured of De Zwaan in Vinkel is this photograph taken in June 1964 by teenager Nico Jurgens, who was very saddened to learn that the beloved mill would be dismantled and sent to America. The blades are in rouwstand (mourning position).* Courtesy of Nico Jurgens.

To express the community's sadness, and in keeping with mill tradition, van Schayk placed the blades of the mill in "rouwstand" (mourning position) when he sold it, a position usually reserved for the death of someone close to the miller or within the miller's family.

On June 11, 1964, Willard Wichers met with van Schayk at De Zwaan. In a gesture captured on film, they slapped palms and sealed the deal with a firm handshake in a traditional Dutch bargaining manner. This was strictly ceremonial, a photo opportunity to share with

*With the slap of the palms and a firm handshake in the traditional Dutch manner of closing a sale, Willard Wichers and De Zwaan's former miller pose for a photograph on June 11, 1964, marking the transfer of the mill, although van Schayk was not actually a party to the sale.* City of Holland, Windmill Island Archives.

*A. J. de Koning, technical advisor to the Dutch Mill Society (left), reviews plans for the reassembly of the mill in Holland so that Diek Medendorp can plan precisely how to disassemble the structure.* City of Holland, Windmill Island Archives

the public back in Holland. The purchase agreement made with the city of Holland did not involve van Schayk, who had previously sold the mill to the millwright firm Gebroeders Adriaens. However, a photograph with the broker would not have been nearly as compelling.

Holland residents learned of the purchase on the same day in the *Holland Evening Sentinel.* The front page headline declared, "Purchase Mill from Netherlands. De Zwaan Located in Vinkel."

*Removing the latticework from the blades was the first step of the disassembly process.* City of Holland, Windmill Island Archives

Reporting from back in his hospital bed in The Hague on Sunday night, June 14, Wichers wrote a letter to the Holland city manager and executive committee explaining the schedule:

*This week, Medendorp moves tools and equipment to Vinkel. Work begins on dismantling which, hopefully, can be completed in 3 weeks. The wings & structural parts are in good condition and will be shipped directly to Rotterdam; the balance to Medendorp's workshop at Zuidlaren for replacement or restoration. Early in September, we hope to have it aboard ship bound for the Great Lakes so that early in October, Medendorp can arrive in Holland, Michigan, to supervise the re-assembly on its new base and get a head start on winter.*

Two days later, the dismantling of De Zwaan began. Wichers made sure that it was captured on film for posterity and for audiences back in the United States. He hired a well-known Dutch film producer who had recently made a film about the restoration of the mill at Keukenhof Gardens, also by millwright Diek Medendorp. Wichers reported the progress in a letter dated June 17. "Max de Haas, with cameras in hand, traveled to Vinkel yesterday to record the first steps in dismantling including the most dramatic, the removal of the wings."

After removing the asphalt siding, Medendorp broke down the mill piece by piece, much in the reverse order of how he would reassemble it. Years later when asked about the condition of De Zwaan when he began to dismantle it, Medendorp explained that he often found mills to be in better shape than expected; however, the condition of De Zwaan was much worse. "Slecht, heel slecht (Bad,

*Diek Medendorp as he worked to disassemble De Zwaan.* City of Holland, Windmill Island Archives

very bad)," he said.

Indeed, Medendorp found that three of the eight main structural upright beams had decayed so much they were unusable and would have to be replaced. He typically saw that kind of decay in poldermolens (water-pumping mills), where the two beams located nearest the water wheel, used to lift the water, wear out from their constant exposure to the water. However De Zwaan had served as a grain mill since its erection in Vinkel in 1884. And before that, according to the Dutch Mill Society, the mill had been built as a hemp mill in Krommenie, North Holland. Medendorp did not have long to ponder this unexpected wear; he had a lot more work to do.

Medendorp also found the spur wheel, which transfers power from the main upright turning shaft outward to the stone gears, in poor condition, as were the stone gears that help drive the turning of the top millstone (called the runner). He was not specific about whether he would custom make new parts or find used parts.

Meanwhile, Wichers kept busy coordinating the details for the shipment. He reported the complicated efforts in another letter to the committee in Holland on June 24:

*This afternoon, had a meeting in Rotterdam with officials of Holland-America and Orange Line. They are most cooperative and agreed to accept and store, at the wharf, parts of the mill which can be sent there directly from Vinkel. Special trucks and loading apparatus will be required for some of the timbers, wings, etc. We also must get a permit for the oversize load and get proper police escort. A firm in Breda is best able to do the job, according to the Holland-America Line people. We meet Captain Glaredorp of the Orange Line to get a first-hand look at the mill parts while in Vinkel tomorrow.*

Knowing how much the committee hoped to have the delivery made directly to Holland so that the community could be on hand to ceremoniously welcome the ship and the mill, Wichers also explained the complicated issues of getting a big cargo vessel into the port of Holland:

*The men doubt whether their ship can put into the Holland Harbor. They point out that the unloading would be a problem because we have no stevedores or cranes. I said we were partially equipped. Will you airmail channel depth and other navigational data as well as what equipment is available for unloading? If Holland is inadequate, hope they will agree to put into Muskegon.*

Once Medendorp had the mill dismantled and most of it shipped to storage in Rotterdam, he began working on restoring certain critical pieces. In Holland, the committee moved forward with the aggressive schedule required in order to open the windmill to the public in just ten months. On July 22, the city offered Jaap de Blecourt the position as head gardener on Windmill Island, and he accepted by telephone from his office at the Grand Hotel on Mackinac Island, where he held a similar post. De Blecourt had

*Former head gardener at the 200-acre grounds of the Grand Hotel on Mackinac Island and formally trained in The Netherlands, Jaap de Blecourt was hired as the head gardener for Windmill Island.* City of Holland, Windmill Island Archives.

degrees from both the College of Floriculture in Aalsmeer and the College of Horticulture in Boskoop, the only man in the previous eighty years to have graduated from both schools. He soon relocated to Holland and began developing plans for elaborate gardens and the planting of more than 100,000 tulips and many other perennials that would bloom in the spring.

The entrance road and mill base were started in August, and Dell Construction of Holland was selected to build the base and would later also be hired to build the service bridge. Work began immediately on site to prepare for the mill's arrival the following month.

In September, the contractors began driving thirty-two forty-foot pilings into the ground to bear the load of the new brick base that would raise the mill thirty feet high to capture the wind. The base would be thirty-four feet in diameter at the ground and slope inward to twenty-eight feet in diameter at its top, where a gallery would serve as the base onto which the mill would be set.

After reviewing the navigational charts for Lake Michigan, the Orange Line made its final decision about which port to enter and it was not the decision that Wichers had hoped for. On September 10, company officials informed Hol-

*The clearing of trees began in July 1964 for development of a road and parking lot for Windmill Island.* City of Holland, Windmill Island Archives.

*In August 1964, bulldozers and graders moved tons of earth to form the ten-foot-high mound on which the windmill would sit.* City of Holland, Windmill Island Archives.

land's mayor, Nelson Bosman, that "it is nautically impossible to use your harbor at Holland."

The shipping company had determined that the Port of Muskegon would be capable of accepting their vessel. The

*In early September 1964, thirty-two pilings were set in a circle and driven about forty feet into the ground to support the brick base and windmill.* City of Holland, Windmill Island Archives.

*The temporary steel tower to use as a guide for laying the brick base was completed by early October and stood ready for inspection by Diek Medendorp who would soon arrive from The Netherlands.* City of Holland, Windmill Island Archives.

steamship line assigned the task of transporting De Zwaan to *Prins Willem van Oranje*, one of many ships named for the Prince William of Orange. The luxurious, 460-foot steel passenger and cargo ship had been launched just eleven years earlier at Bolnes, The Netherlands, as hull number 949 by Boele's Schepsverken & Machinefabriek shipbuilders for the Orange Line.

Since the recent opening of the St. Lawrence Seaway, that ship, along with others belonging to Oranje Lijn, was used for travel between Rotterdam and the United States. It would leave Rotterdam with its precious cargo in early September.

Under the guidance of Captain Aart Schuijer, the ship arrived safely into the Muskegon harbor on the morning of Monday, October 5, 1964. Heavy shipping traffic in the St. Lawrence Seaway had slowed its trip through the Great Lakes. Then, after scheduled stops in Toronto, Cleveland, and Detroit, rough seas on Lake Huron and Lake Michigan further delayed the much-anticipated arrival.

A delegation from Holland met the *Prins Willem van Oranje* in Muskegon. They watched as the Dutch sailors began carefully unloading the windmill parts and transferring them to five flatbed trucks, one trailer, and a rig for the eighty-foot blades of the windmill. The windmill committee had been successful in obtaining participation from several trucking companies, including Associated Truck Lines, Holland Motor Express, Michigan Express, Roadway Express, Rooks Transfer, Wolverine Express, and the Wm. Mokma Movers and Riggers, which handled the difficult transportation of the huge blades.

A formal ceremony on board the ship

*De Zwaan's blades, too large to be crated, were removed with a crane and loaded onto waiting trucks.* City of Holland, Windmill Island Archives.

*The mill amounted to about seventy tons of parts.* Holland Museum Archives.

began at 4:00 p.m. Participants included the windmill committee, Holland city officials, representatives of the Dutch government, and members of the Muskegon City Council and Muskegon Chamber of Commerce. There were speeches and exchanges of flowers, and young ladies from Holland wearing traditional Dutch costumes presented decorated wooden shoes to the captain. On behalf of the Dutch Mill Society, Captain Schuijer presented a Dutch flag to fly alongside the American flag over the windmill. In return, Carter Brown presented scrolls to the captain to be given to those instrumental in the windmill negotiation

*Willard Wichers and Carter Brown (at left) accepted custody of De Zwaan at a ceremony on board the ship. They presented scrolls of appreciation to Captain Aart Schuijer and H.M. Holden, Chicago agent for the Orange Line. Reverend Jan Verkuylen, (seated) offered the benediction.* City of Holland, Windmill Island Archives.

process back in The Netherlands. Reverend Jan Verkuylen, a visiting professor of theology at Nazareth College in Kalamazoo, delivered an invocation and blessing. The windmill committee could not have selected a better person to conclude the ceremony. The Dutch professor had been born less than a mile from De Zwaan in Vinkel and knew the miller van Schayk. Like other Dutch individuals, the reverend was not in favor of De Zwaan leaving The Netherlands, but as plans developed he accepted it as an appropriate way to honor Holland's Dutch roots. In fact, Mayor Bosman followed up with a thank-you letter that contained a most prophetic statement: "We can sympathize with the regret felt by the good people of Vinkel who lost their mill and will trust that in time they will feel a deep bond with the people of Holland who will share with them their affection for De Zwaan."

After the ceremony, the committee arranged a buffet on board the ship for the delegation as a celebration of a successful journey across the ocean and of the acceptance of the long-awaited mill on behalf of the people of Holland. As photographs of the party attest, participants, as well as the captain, had a wonderful time.

The celebration for the ship's arrival in Muskegon had been grand, but the committee planned an even more spectacular celebration for De Zwaan's arrival in Holland. As an early winter storm blew in, the caravan of seven local trucks left Muskegon at 3:00 p.m. on Tuesday, escorted by the Muskegon police and state police. Ottawa County sheriff's officers took over at the county line and escorted the trucks into Holland. There the caravan joined the parade procession, including a Boy Scout color guard, National Guard vehicles, the Holland Fire

*Photographs taken on board the* **Prins Willem van Oranje** *offer a glimpse of the festivities.* Holland Museum Archives.

Department ladder truck, an historic vehicle belonging to the Allegan Farm Power Company, Miss Holland Bonnie Timmer, and cars with members of the windmill committee. The participation of two local high school bands had to be canceled due to the inclement weather, and so police sirens took the place of marching bands.

*The day after its arrival, De Zwaan, loaded in several trucks and flatbeds was paraded down Eighth Street in Holland.* City of Holland, Windmill Island Archives.

The parade began at Lincoln Street and headed west on Eighth Street ceremoniously leading the trucks, several bearing signs declaring "America's Only Authentic Dutch Windmill," to the Civic Center. By then, it must have been forgotten that another authentic Dutch windmill still stood on the Kellogg estate at Gull Lake. There was some disappointment among the crowd when all they saw were trucks and not actually a windmill. Many months would pass before they would see the windmill reassembled at its new home.

The next morning, the trucks delivered the windmill to the Holland municipal warehouse and garage located at Fairbanks Avenue (the site of the DeVos Fieldhouse today), where the city crane assisted in removing the huge millstones, blades, and the many other pieces, including the center shaft.

Work on the island continued. De Forest Excavating began construction of the parking lot. Willard Meyer was hired to build the canal, dikes, and drawbridge. Amid all this activity, millwright Diek Medendorp arrived with his wife on

*The parade festivities drew to a close at the Holland Civic Center.* City of Holland, Windmill Island Archives.

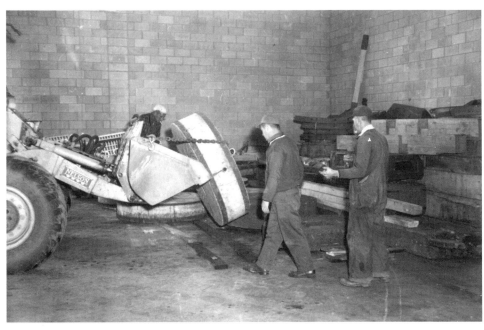

*(Right) Parts of De Zwaan were unloaded into the municipal warehouse where Diek Medendorp began preparation work to reassemble the windmill. Some of the thirty-foot main structural beams, well over a hundred years old, did not pass his inspection. He is pictured notching out a replacement beam.* City of Holland, Windmill Island Archives.

*(Below) Diek Medendorp conferred with Willard Wichers and Jaap de Blecourt, who developed the design of the garden plantings.* City of Holland, Windmill Island Archives.

Saturday, October 10, and knew he had his work cut out for him. He wasted no time in getting to the warehouse to look over the mill parts stored there and then visited the site on which he would reassemble the mill. The couple settled into an apartment at the Warm Friend Hotel on Eighth Street, where they would be staying over the next many months.

Medendorp began his work promptly on Monday morning, while Dell Construction started the process of laying the three-story brick base. Made in America, the red bricks matched as much as possible a brick that had been flown over from The Netherlands as representative of the material used in Dutch windmills. The bricks were laid in a manner typical of Dutch building, applying a slight outward slant for bearing the load above as well as allowing water to shed easily to ensure that the mill would stay dry, an important concern for a grain mill. The construction of the base took place over the balance of October, November, and half of December, during a period when early snows made the work more difficult. Sitework continued for as long as the weather allowed.

On a cold and blustery December 14, 1964, city officials, windmill committee members, a National Guard Color Guard, and Miss Holland Bonnie Timmer, dressed in Dutch costume, held a ceremony marking the first placement by crane of the main structural members of the mill. Workers at the site expressed concern that the wind would complicate the mounting process, but the process went smoothly. They raised the two forty-two-foot-high, flat-topped A-frames

*In mid-October masons began laying the bricks to form the octagon base for De Zwaan.* City of Holland, Windmill Island Archives.

*By mid-December 1964, the brick base and supports for the gallery were completed and landscaping was under way.* City of Holland, Windmill Island Archives.

*On December 14, 1964, Diek Metdendorp oversaw the placement of the first huge A-frame that formed the mill body. A brief ceremony took place that day to mark this significant step.* City of Holland, Windmill Island Archives.

and two smaller cross frames and set them upon the base to form the sides of the windmill. Once in place, each frame was tied to the ground by steel cables and bolted to heavy angle irons fastened to the cross-beams.

The next morning, despite heavy snowfall, workmen hoisted the two large millstones to the top of the mill's base. The stones were not mounted in their permanent positions, but they had to be placed inside of the superstructure before the framework was completed, because it would be impossible to insert them afterwards. Medendorp then mounted corner posts and girders for the mill's octagonal sides.

By early February 1965, the mill stood in the middle of a wintry wasteland. Medendorp and his workmen kept busy inside, constructing five floors within the mill's shell and installing the stairways. Weather soon allowed the carpenters to begin installing the 30,000 one-inch-thick, hand-hewn shingles, and by the end of the month, the mill had been fully clad.

In early March, workmen began driving pilings that would support the Dutch drawbridge designed as a replica of a bridge that once spanned the Amstel River in The Netherlands to serve pedestrian traffic to the island, as well as the service bridge for maintenance vehicles. The committee had previously decided that no passenger vehicles would be allowed on the island.

*Diek Medendorp worked on the wooden brake wheel that drives the center shaft to prepare it for reinstallation in De Zwaan.* City of Holland, Windmill Island Archives.

*The mill skeleton had been erected by late December 1964.* City of Holland, Windmill Island Archives.

*By the end of 1964, the skeleton of the mill had been clad and the application of some 30,000, one-inch-thick, hand-hewn cedar shingles began.* Holland Museum Archives.

*Workmen continued outfitting the inside of the mill during the coldest days of January and February 1965.* Holland Museum Archives.

*The wind shaft for the sail stocks was hoisted into position through the framework of the uncompleted cap.* City of Holland, Windmill Island Archives.

*(Opposite) Work on the bridge and post house was accelerated as dedication day loomed ahead.* Holland Museum Archives.

*(Opposite) Maynard Schrotenboer of Dell Construction attached a winch to one of De Zwaan's four millstones, which had been hoisted into the mill before it was completed.* City of Holland, Windmill Island Archives.

Construction also began on the post house, another replica structure. The building would house the administration offices, information station, canteen food service, and gift shop where visitors could purchase souvenirs and packaged flour ground by De Zwaan.

On March 11, the public learned that the date for the windmill's dedication had been set for April 10, nearly a month before the planned completion by Tulip Time, to coincide with the visit of Prince Bernhard of The Netherlands to Detroit. His Royal Highness agreed to schedule a day trip to Holland to help dedicate De Zwaan. By that time, the first Windmill Island brochure had been designed, and the city ordered 200,000 copies to be ready for the dedication.

*Diek Medendorp was introduced by Willard Wichers to H. A. Hoogendoorn, from the Embassy for Press and Cultural Affairs for The Netherlands, who was visiting Hope College.* City of Holland, Windmill Island Archives.

With that significant deadline looming, the pace of construction quickened. On March 15, the two-ton platform on which the cap would rest was hoisted into place atop the main structure of the mill. Then, in the following days, Mendendorp installed the copper cap piece-by-piece. On March 26, just two weeks before the dedication, the first of the blades was hoisted into place. Diek Medendorp took a few moments to meet with a *Holland Senti-nel* reporter to point out the bullet holes in the eighty-foot blade, which had been battered by heavy bombardment during World War II. De Zwaan looked more like its old self after construction workers finished placing the second blade. Installing the wooden lattice work of the blades took the better part of those next two weeks. De Zwaan was ready just in time for the arrival of Prince Bernhard and the long-anticipated dedication day.

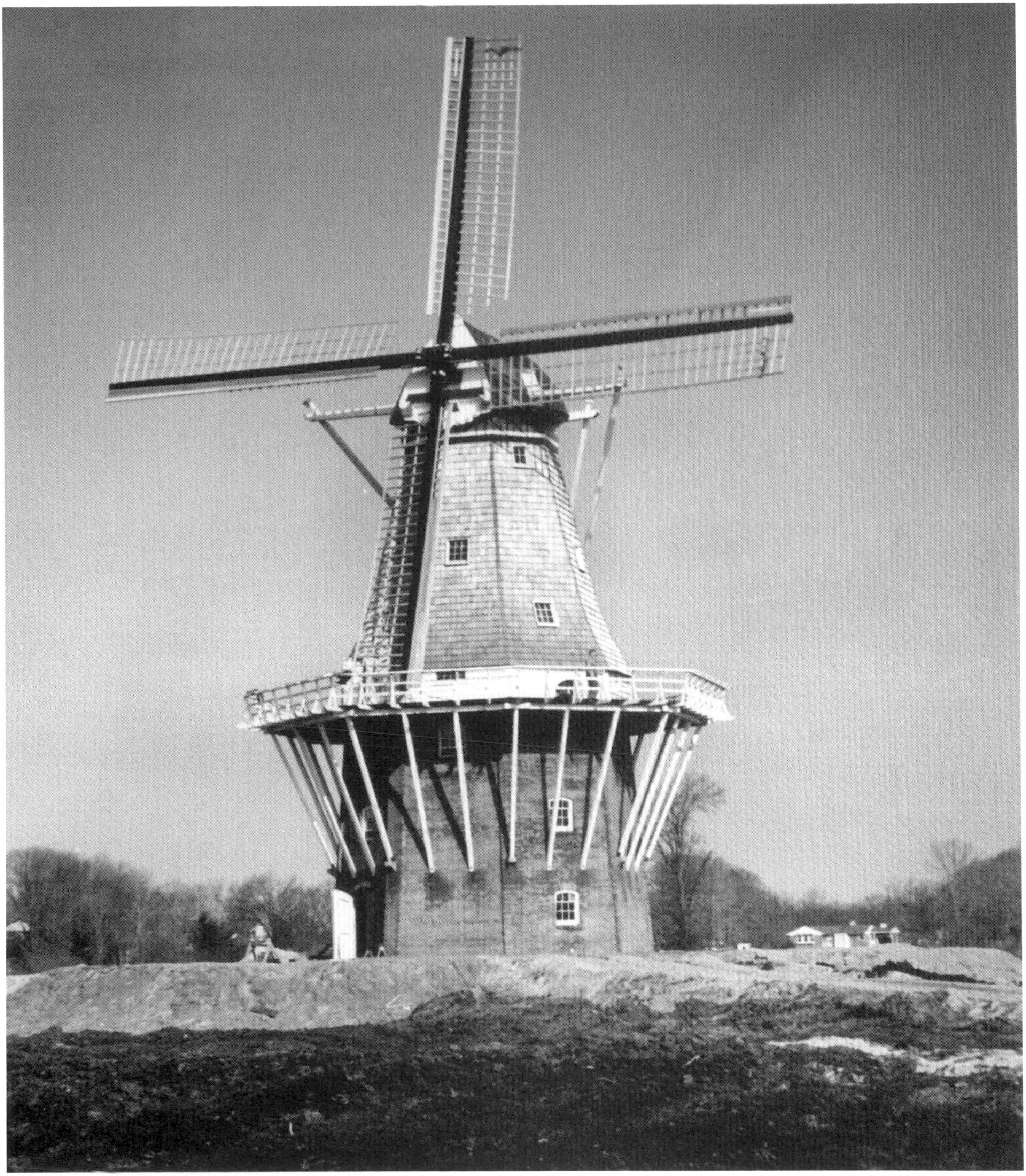

# Premiere Tourist Attraction

On the overcast morning of April 10, 1965, a delegation of Project Windmill officials met Prince Bernhard of The Netherlands at the Muskegon Airport, where hundreds of people had gathered to catch a glimpse of His Royal Highness. The prince, a private pilot, had actually flown the last leg of the trip from Detroit to Muskegon himself. It would be a long and busy day for all with a schedule of events in Holland that began at 9:00 a.m. and did not end for the prince until late that night. Everything was conducted with great ceremony and respect for the momentous occasion of both a royal visit and the dedication of the long-awaited windmill.

At 10:00 a.m., the prince arrived at Graves Hall at Hope College, where he participated in a press conference. Dozens of news reporters from the wire services, newspapers, and radio and television stations ensured that there was state, national, and international coverage of the dedication and Prince Bernhard's activities that day. Through the studios of WHTC and by overseas phone connections, Dutch correspondent Willebroad Nieuwenhuis for radio and television station KRO broadcast live, airing it on all four major networks in The Netherlands. The press conference was followed by a convocation at Dimnent Chapel on the campus, where the prince delivered a speech titled "International Understanding and Individual Responsibility." At 12:45 p.m., the entourage attended a luncheon at the college's Phelps Hall, where Michigan governor George Romney, who had flown into Park Township airport earlier that morning, joined the prince, the Windmill Committee, other dignitaries, and invited guests.

*Some six hundred people gathered at 2:30 p.m. on Saturday, April 10, 1965, for a ceremony to dedicate the relocation of De Zwaan windmill, beginning a long run as a premier tourist attraction in Michigan.* Holland Museum Archives.

*Prince Bernhard flew into Muskegon and greeted well-wishers there.* Holland Museum Archives.

After the luncheon, the group was transported to Windmill Island in convertibles. From the island parking lot, the National Guard Color Guard led the official party on foot to the drawbridge where Hope College freshman Linda Pat-

*Events in Holland on Saturday included a press conference in Graves Hall on the Hope College campus.* City of Holland, Windmill Island Archives.

*Prince Bernhard delivered an address at Dimnent Chapel called "International Understanding - Individual Responsibility."* City of Holland, Windmill Island Archives.

*Hope College freshman Linda Patterson sold the first visa (admission ticket) for Windmill Island to Prince Bernhard at the drawbridge. Governor George Romney stands between them.* City of Holland, Windmill Island Archives.

terson, in Dutch costume, greeted them and sold the first visa, the name for an admission ticket, to the prince. He paid the value of 3.6 guilders with a 10-guilder note, but Miss Patterson told him she did not have change for a guilder. With a chuckle, Prince Bernhard offered to pay for Governor Romney, too, and told her to keep the change.

Over six hundred people followed the prince, purchasing their own tickets, and by 2:30 p.m. everyone had gathered at the base of De Zwaan where the Dutch and United States national anthems were played. The Reverend Russell Vande Bunte of Third Reformed Church offered a dedicatory prayer, and James Malcolm of the Hope College drama department took over as the master of ceremonies. He introduced Governor Romney, who made a short speech, and then Prince Bernhard, who spoke briefly about the relationship between the two countries. The prince then presented Carter Brown, the man who four years earlier had proposed erecting a windmill, with a treasured old map of the Zaan District showing the location of De Zwaan before it was moved to Vinkel. He also presented a bottle of water from the Zaan River,

*(Below and opposite) Prince Bernhard delivers a brief speech to dedicate De Zwaan.* City of Holland, Windmill Island Archives.

which had once flowed past De Zwaan, "so that De Zwaan would always be near some part of its homeland."

An interesting back story to that bottle of water would have unexpected repercussions just weeks later, though no one would hear about it for a half century, until the publication of this book. In preparation for the dedication, Willard Wichers had weeks earlier contacted government authorities in the Zaan District to tell them about Holland's recent acquisition of De Zwaan, which had once stood in their region, and to request a bottle of river water to be used by Prince Bernhard in "christening" the relocated windmill. The local authorities in Zaan, who had not been aware of De Zwaan's relocation until then, were immediately concerned about Prince Bernhard's reputation. They knew that the Dutch never used water to dedicate a windmill; it was traditional to release the brake to set the blades in motion. They agreed to send the

water as a souvenir from the Zaan District so long as it was not used in a way that would embarrass the prince. Wichers readily agreed to change his plans for the dedication ceremonies to include the traditional brake release. Unbeknownst to him at the time, his news about De Zwaan prompted immediate discussions about the mill among government officials in the Zaan District, the results of which will be revealed in Chapter 7.

After the speeches, Governor Romney, Prince Bernhard, and select members of the delegation climbed the stairs inside the mill to the gallery where they met Diek Medendorp, who quickly provided instructions about the temporary system he had rigged for the ceremonial pulling of the brake. The prince pulled on the rope but the blades didn't move, and the governor reached up to help tug on it. With the efforts of both men, the brake was released and the blades began to turn, but the force of their joint pull broke a temporary two-by-four meant to simulate the brake pole. Fortunately, most of those in attendance were fixed

*Together Governor George Romney and Prince Bernhard released the brake to set the blades in motion, the typical Dutch tradition to dedicate a windmill.*
City of Holland, Windmill Island Archives.

on the anticipation of seeing the blades turn and did not notice what actually happened high up on the gallery. The temporary brake pole came tumbling down, narrowly missing the prince but hitting Carter Brown on the shoulder and tearing his coat. Fortunately, he was not seriously hurt, and that was the only mishap of the day. Had the prince been struck instead, Holland might have faced an embarrassing international incident.

After the ceremony, the dignitaries were led by a parade from the island down Eighth Street to the Civic Center for a Koffe-Kletz where the prince was honored. More than 450 guests from the surrounding local governments partici-

*Immediately following the dedication, a parade began at the island, headed down Eighth Street and reached the Civic Center, where refreshments were served (below).* City of Holland, Windmill Island Archives.

pated. Another 175 other people attended a private stag dinner that evening at the Point West Restaurant on the south side of Lake Macatawa by Lake Michigan. After a full day, Prince Bernhard returned to Detroit late that night.

One week after the dedication, Willard Wichers escorted Diek Medendorp to New York City to appear on the popular, long-running panel game show "What's My Line," which had been airing since 1950. Hosted by John Charles Daly, the game tasked celebrity panelists with questioning contestants in order to determine their occupations. Months earlier, Wichers had written the show's producers proposing Medendorp as a guest, hoping to garner national attention for the new windmill. The episode ran on Sunday evening April 18, with panelists Arlene Francis, Abe Burrows, Anita Gillette, and Bennett Cerf.

Like all the contestants, Medendorp was invited to enter and sign in on the chalk board. Daly asked him where he was from and it immediately became clear that English was not his first language. "I come from Zuidlaren in The Nederlands," he said nervously, "and I work now in Holland, Michigan."

Daly invited him to take a seat next to him, opposite the panelists, and then let the audience at home know of Medendorp's occupation through words on the screen: "Repairs and Restores Windmills." Then Daly provided a bit of information to set the questioning in the right direction. "Mr. Medendorp is self-employed, deals in a service, and we will admit that there is a product associated with it."

He invited Bennett Cerf to begin, letting the audience know the panelists would be allowed ten questions. Acknowledging both The Netherlands' association with

*The appearance of Diek Medendorp on the CBS television game show "What's My Line" was arranged by Willard Wichers to get national promotion for Windmill Island.*
Jack van Heest collection.

cheese, as well as Michigan's, Cerf asked if he had anything to do with cheese. "No," Medendorp said, shaking his head from side to side.

The other panelists pursued such questions as whether he had any connection to flowers, or worked directly with the public. Eventually the questions led Medendorp to admit that he worked sometimes indoors and sometimes outside, and that he often worked elevated above the ground, did mechanical work, and typically wore work clothes, not a suit. Arlene Francis garnered quite a laugh after Medendorp acknowledged that he "is very active during work." She replied, "And on the seventh day you rest."

By the ninth question, Bennett Cerf had caught on. "Mr. Medendorp, can I eliminate something that is very famous in The Netherlands—windmills?"

As the audience laughed, Daly replied, "No, you can't!" He then explained to the panelists that Medendorp built and restored windmills and had been erecting a mill called De Zwaan in Holland, Michigan. Without missing a beat, Bennett Cerf took the opportunity to tease the host. He asked the millwright, "Do you feel a big wind right where you are sitting now?"

Although Medendorp didn't seem to understand the question, he nodded his head in affirmation, and the audience roared!

The power of television was readily apparent at Tulip Time that year. Thousands of people came inquiring about the new "star" millwright, Mr. Medendorp.

While Medendorp and Wichers were in New York for the show, work continued at Windmill Island on the post house. Medendorp had brought the concept of that structure to the city of Holland. He had been working on a windmill in Ruinen, Drenthe, when he learned of the restoration of a 300-year-old post house in Ruinen and thought that such a building would serve the needs of Holland. The city acquired the plans for the post house through the mayor of Ruinen at a cost of about $300 and selected a contractor to build the replica for $55,000. It was designed as a modified H-shaped structure with the main part being sixty-three by thirty feet and the smaller section forty-two by twenty feet. Historically a post house would have served travelers as a place to eat and rest, as well as to stable their horses. At Windmill Island, the main section was designed to house restrooms, a lobby, and information desk, while the smaller part was to serve as a concession area for visitors. The connecting wing would be used for staff offices.

The question of whether to operate Windmill Island six days or seven days a week had been highly controversial, and as the public opening date loomed, a final decision had to be made. At an early March city council meeting, letters from fourteen city and area churches that opposed the Sunday operation had been read, and a petition with 1,959 signatures was presented. Others who opposed the Sunday operation suggested a compromise, proposing that Windmill Island

*A replica of a 300-year-old post house in Ruinen, The Netherlands, this building originally served for a visitor center, concessions, and staff offices.* Author's Collection.

could be "open on Sundays, provided no fees or admissions were charged, and that the facilities be used to give expression to the Christian faith of the community." A resident, Mrs. William Westrate, raised the question of whether revenues would be sufficient to meet the bonds that had been sold to finance the project. Councilman Morris Peerbolt pointed out that the projected revenue, based on the tourism study by Dr. Frank Suggitt, was for a six-days-a-week operation. They had decided to table the decision until after the upcoming city election in April, because, as Councilman Eugene Vande Vusse pointed out, the makeup of the council would change.

By the third week in April, the new council voted seven to two in favor of Sunday operations of Windmill Island. As reported by the *Detroit Free Press*, "The seven-days-a-week operation had been recommended by the windmill committee. Sunday programs will emphasize cultural aspects of the community and information on its Dutch heritage. Musical selections and choral groups will replace performances by klompen danc-ers." Daily admission fees were set at $1 for adults and .50 cents for children.

Windmill Island opened officially on Saturday, May 8, 1965. Arie de Koning, technical advisor for the Dutch Mill Society, traveled from The Netherlands to attend. He and Diek Medendorp were anxious to take a close look at the mill's brake, which they had not yet perfected. Unfortunately, they found some technical difficulties with the system and had to cancel flour milling operations that day. However, Medendorp somehow managed to have the blades turn about five minutes every half hour so that visitors could catch a glimpse of De Zwaan in motion. The opening weekend was intended to be "Holland weekend," encouraging the local community to come and see the newest attraction, but out-of-state visitors wanted a chance to view De Zwaan too. In all, more than 4,000 people visited Windmill Island the first weekend, twice as many on Sunday as Saturday, with 90 percent of the visitors from out of state.

Windmill Island manager Jerry Fairbanks admitted that the large crowd dur-

*Diek Medendorp returned to Holland where he spent the summer of 1965 as De Zwaan's miller. He is pictured loading grain into the hopper on the stone floor.* Author's Collection.

play in this region, if not in the country." De Blecourt had the help of Jacob De-Graaf, the head of the city's Parks Department, and the technical advice of Willem van der Lee, the Dutch landscape architect who had designed the famous Keukenhof Gardens in Lisse.

Diek Medendorp was able to solve the issues with the brake system and succeeded in grinding the first flour by Wednesday afternoon at four o'clock. The blades of the mill turned in the fifteen-mile-per-hour wind, but his initial grinding only lasted fifteen minutes. The first two-pound bag of whole wheat flour was ceremoniously presented to Mayor Nelson Bosman by Nellie Medendorp, in the presence of her husband and Arie de Koning.

Before daylight on Saturday morning, Medendorp had ground almost a ton of flour, which he put into two-pound bags. Every bag sold at the post house during the Tulip Time weekend. Willard Wichers did his part that busy weekend, selling tickets from the ticket booth to help keep the line of cars moving. The 300-space parking lot filled up, and the shuttle service from Warm Friend Hotel had difficulty getting through the traffic; more than 3,000 people walked to the island from town. The island had almost 22,000 visitors during the weekend. The well-timed tulips, the favorable weather, the entertaining klompen dancers, and De Zwaan all served to draw a record-breaking crowd that year. After the first nine days of operation, 40,000 people had visited Windmill Island.

Following Tulip Time, on May 17 the Holland City Council, the Windmill Committee, Windmill Island staff, and city department heads attended a special showing of the uncut film footage taken of the negotiations, selection, and disman-

ing the opening weekend "was a good shakedown for the staff, and we learned a lot which will serve us well during Tulip Time." The staff only had Monday and Tuesday to catch their breath since the Tulip Time Festival began on Wednesday, May 12, and ran through Saturday, May 15.

The 125,000 tulip bulbs that Jaap de Blecourt planted the prior fall bloomed beautifully, creating a park setting reminiscent of The Netherlands. The island became, as City Manager Herbert Holt had predicted when de Blecourt was hired, "the outstanding horticultural dis-

tling of De Zwaan in The Netherlands. With no sound track, Willard Wichers narrated, explaining that Time Life had been contracted by the city to edit the three-and-a-half hours of footage down to a thirty-minute film suitable for television and presentation at the island. The film was followed by a question-and-answer session with Arie de Koning and Diek Medendorp. The highlight of the evening came at the intermission when de Koning presented a beautiful, artistic scroll to the city of Holland, accepted by Carter Brown on behalf of the Windmill Committee. The words on the scroll read:

*Impressed highly by the execution of the Windmill Island project in Holland, Michigan,*

*Wherein the Dutch windmill demolished in the old country of the Province of North Brabant, the Village of Vinkel, sailed over to Holland, Michigan to fulfill a central position,*

*Convinced that the project and especially the windmill accentuate the bonds of history and affection between both Holland here and over there,*

*Wishes to honour the American Friends of our Society in the person of the author intellectualis of the magnificent project – Mr. Carter P. Brown, Chairman of the Committee for his splendid initiative and endeavour related to this work,*

*The work appealing to the best historical traditional linking our people here and over there,*

*The work that in the years to come might be the symbol of friendship and mutual admiration.*

*De Hollandsche Molen*
*Vereniging tot behoud van molens*
*in Nederland*
*Amsterdam, October 1964*

That evening also served as a farewell to Arie de Koning and to Nellie Medendorp, who had been living in Holland with her husband since October 1964. They would leave for The Netherlands the following day along with Diek Medendorp, but Diek would be returning after ten days with an extension of his visa so that he could serve as miller for the duration of the summer. The Windmill Committee had, thus far, not found a person to serve in that capacity despite a creative radio appeal to finding a miller, publicized the previous October:

*If you're hip on your kiddie literature, you'll remember the Little Red Hen had trouble finding someone to help her grind wheat. There's a swan in Holland, Michigan, with something of the same problem.*

*Holland has imported an authentic Dutch windmill, a 200-year-old granddaddy that goes by the name of "De Zwaan." The trouble is, when city fathers bought De Zwaan from the Netherlands, they neglected to ask for a miller too. Now it appears that only an experienced Dutch windmill miller can operate De Zwaan and give it the care it's accustomed to. And genuine Dutch millers in the U.S. are about as scarce as Sioux Indians in Amsterdam.*

*Holland's De Zwaan has eight 5-foot grindstones. When they're finished with a load of wheat or corn, the result should be flour. De Zwaan also has a 30-foot-high brick foundation and 80-foot sails. That's way up there in the middle of the air, and when a storm blows in from Lake Michigan across the broad acres of Holland somebody better be on hand who knows how to head the sails into the wind and do whatever else is necessary to keep De Zwaan from singing its swan song. That's a job for a miller, the real McDutch.*

*Willard C. Wichers, Midwest Director of Information for the Netherlands, is combing the files of his office in the Tulip City to locate a Dutch immigrant with windmill milling experience. This is one time when a run-of-the-mill person is just what's needed.*

The search for a person with milling experience turned up three potential candidates. Holland resident Theo Voetberg, who was sixty-six years old and retired when the mill arrived in Holland, was from Schroterland, Friesland, and had apparently operated three windmills in The Netherlands. Wichers had several conversations with Henry Vander Werf from nearby Hudsonville, who had worked for the Dutch Mill Society as a millwright maintaining and restoring mills, under the direction of Arie de Koning, before coming to the United States in 1947. He also talked to Andrew Rienstra, who lived on a farm east of Holland and who had been a miller in The Netherlands before immigrating to America in 1914. However, all were seniors and operating De Zwaan would be a strenuous job.

In late May, the *Holland Evening Sentinel* reported that "Details have been cleared with immigration departments to allow Medendorp to return here for the season and serve as miller in windmill De Zwaan. During his absence, no flour has been milled. Production will resume on his return. Windmill Island officials said Holland is most grateful that Medendorp could return to serve as miller for the season."

He arrived just in time for the Memorial Day weekend, put De Zwaan back into operation, and quickly ground enough flour to meet the weekend demand

of about 300 two-pound bags. Almost 2,800 people visited the island during the holiday weekend, representing nineteen states plus Canada and Germany. The largest crowds had come on Sunday, despite the shortened hours of 11:30 a.m. to 6:30 p.m., making it clear that the Holland City Council had made the right choice for a seven-day operation.

During that first season, Maynard Schrotenboer, who had worked with his brother Del of Dell Construction erecting De Zwaan, assisted Medendrop with the milling. By the end of the summer, Schrotenboer agreed to serve as the seasonal miller beginning the next spring.

As partial compensation for his work, the city of Holland, with the help of Robert DeNooyer of DeNooyer Chevrolet and Myron van Oort, shipped a Malibu convertible to Medendorp in The Netherlands, to replace the Corvair DeNooyer had loaned him while he lived in Holland. In return for DeNooyer's friendship during his stay in Holland, Medendorp crafted a one-tenth-size replica of De Zwaan, which DeNooyer later donated to Windmill Island so that many people could enjoy it.

The Windmill Committee planned to expand the attractions on the island the following year by building a replica Friesian farmhouse and barn, like the one from Midlum, The Netherlands, which had been relocated to the Openluchtmuseum in Arnhem in 1963. Although the history of the farm dated to 1644, the house, made of yellow Ijssel brick with glazed black roofing tiles, and the barn, with a thatched roof, was updated and enlarged in 1778. By 1867, the farmhouse was home to a family of eight, plus their two farmhands and two maids. The German migrant workers slept in the barn with the horses. Dr.

states and many foreign countries.

A teacher at the Holland Public Schools joined the staff that summer and for many Tulip Times thereafter. Al McGeehan welcomed guests on the public address system, conducted tours of the windmill, and demonstrated the drawbridge opening. He would later serve from 1993 to 2009 as Holland's longest-term mayor, greatly involved in the operation of Windmill Island.

By October 1965, the Windmill Committee and staff of Windmill Island celebrated a successful first year.

Jerry Fairbanks did not return to Windmill Island for the second season, and Jaap de Blecourt was promoted to manager on March 1, 1966. In the two months prior to the season opening on April 30, de Blecourt oversaw a new coat of paint on the doors and trim of De Zwaan and the installation of new paving bricks by the entrance doors. On the interior, a stainless steel storage bin made in Salinas, Kansas, capable of holding 4,400 pounds of freshly ground flour, was added, as well as an alarm system and new electrical wiring.

In January 1966, Wichers began inquiring of the Dutch Mill Society whether it would permit Medendorp to return to Holland at the beginning of the season in

*De Zwaan was decked out in traditional decorations when Willard Wichers' daughter Janet got married in August 1965. Diek Medendorp strung the symbols on the blades as a thank-you to Wichers, who had played such an important role in acquiring the windmill.* City of Holland, Windmill Island Archives.

A. J. Bernet Kempers, director of the Openluchtmuseum, provided information and plans for the Friesian structures, but after taking bids to build the replica, the city decided to postpone the project due to the cost.

The Windmill Committee received an offer to relocate a nearby wood barn built by a Dutch immigrant in the 1880s, but Willard Wichers did not support the idea because he was "not certain that it was really built in a genuine Dutch style."

During the first year, 117,000 visitors—an average of 650 people per day—flocked to Windmill Island from forty-six

*The city of Holland wanted to construct a replica of an authentic Friesian farmhouse on display at the Openluchtmuseum in Arnhem, The Netherlands. The project never happened due to budget considerations.* Courtesy of Openluchtmuseum.

order to provide additional training to miller Maynard Schrotenboer. Wichers was very much aware that any length of time that Medendorp spent in America meant an interruption and delay in the many restoration projects of windmills in The Netherlands, which only had a small number of skilled millwrights. He conveyed to society officials that whatever arrangements were made, he wanted to be in full cooperation with the wishes and recommendations of the Dutch Mill Society.

Wichers received a response from Frederick Stokhuyzen, president of the Dutch Mill Society, in mid-March. "We are touched by the expression of the feelings of you and your Committee in doing nothing else as in complete agreement with the policy and the wishes of our Society regarding the visit of Mr. Medendorp," he noted. "Our idea on the matter is that we quite agree that Mr. Medendorp goes to Holland, Michigan, in the beginning of May for a period of 2 to 3 weeks for additional instructions to Maynard Schrotenboer." However, Stokhuyzen made an even more generous offer. "The best thing would be that Maynard Schrotenboer should come to the Netherlands for a follow up during the winter months … A stage here in different grain mills would make an all-round miller of him so that there is no further necessity then for you to call on the help of Medendorp. We can sponsor all for Mr. Schrotenboer here and bring him to the different addresses where he can have his practical job during these winter months."

Stokhuyzen closed the letter by noting that "I asked one of the members of our Committee to clear now the question of the history of De Zwaan (together with Mr. Medendorp) and I hope to write you the result in short time." Apparently Wichers was following through with his

desire to learn more about the windmill.

Despite the gracious offer from the Dutch Mill Society, the city of Holland chose not to send Schrontenboer to The Netherlands for training, but hosted another stay by Medendorp. Forty years would pass before Holland would accept a similar offer, but that story will be saved for Chapter 6.

In the summer of 1966, the city purchased the miniature Dutch village exhibit Klein Nederland (Little Netherlands) and had it moved from where it had stood for nearly thirty years in a walled enclosure next to the Netherlands Museum. The exhibit had been built in 1937 by Sipp Houtman and a group of local craftsmen who called themselves the Happy Hobbyists. To house the miniature village, three Zaan-

*Staff are seen here receiving bags of grain to begin the milling process.* City of Holland, Windmill Island Archives.

dam houses were built east of De Zwaan in a style similar to the colorful, often green, buildings common in the Zaan District. In addition, a structure mimicking an architectural detail from the back of the Royal Orphanage in Buren, Gelderland, established in 1613 by Princess Mary, daughter of Prince William of Orange, was built south of the Zaandam houses to serve as concessions. That building freed up the post house where the thirty-minute film about De Zwaan, which had just been completed, could be played.

Maynard Schrotenboer served as the miller for the second and third seasons, but accepted a position with the Holland City Hospital, and later the Holland Police Department, to assure year-round employment. Island manager de Blecourt then faced the challenge of finding another miller for De Zwaan.

De Blecourt had recently visited Colonial Williamsburg in Virginia, and that visit would prove fortuitous. He had fallen into a conversation with John Heuvel, a young Dutch immigrant working alongside his father in the cabinet makers' shop at the heritage site. The vanden

Heuvel family had emigrated from their home town of Hillgersberg, located near Rotterdam, in 1955 when John was just sixteen. Heuvel had shown interest in De Zwaan, and suggested that de Blecourt call him if he needed a man with his talents. In 1968, such an opportunity arose, and de Blecourt offered him the job. Heuvel (who had shortened his name from Johannes vanden Heuvel) packed up his American bride, Marie, and four children and moved to Holland, Michigan, to learn the trade of milling.

The city arranged for Diek Medendorp to return in May 1968 to train Heuvel in the operation of De Zwaan and the dressing (sharpening) of the millstones, as well as to supervise the repairs needed on the mill, including the koningspil (central drive shaft), which had a large crack in it. This was an important repair that only a trained millwright could do.

In 1968 Wichers and the Windmill Committee revisited items that had been included in the master plan for the island. They discussed the construction of a church, for which they had received offers from local masons, but Wichers made

*In 1966 the city of Holland erected three Zaandam houses in which to display the miniature Dutch village, Klein Nederland, acquired from the Holland Museum. The scale model De Zwaan made by Diek Medendorp and donated by Robert DeNooyer can be seen in the background.* City of Holland, Windmill Island Archives.

it clear that the island portion should be reserved for authentic structures from The Netherlands, and replica buildings should stay near the post house. They also discussed the possibility of erecting a small poldermolen to pump water. The committee was willing to entertain the idea of having Medendorp assemble a poldermolen from various parts of other mills that he had, including the base from a mill that originally stood at Hoogkerk. However, Wichers expressed concern about this plan in a letter to Carter Brown in mid-February 1968, stating that "Medendorp's mill is nothing more than an assemblage of parts from many mills and has no particular historical significance."

Wichers continued in his objection, noting, "This has nothing to do with the more profound question of a credibility gap which may arise from our loud proclamations that this was the last mill that would be exported from The Netherlands. I would much prefer them to consider the mill on the Kellogg estate."

Wichers had been investigating the possibility of acquiring the poldermolen that W. K. Kellogg had purchased for his estate in 1927 through contacts in Friesland, from where it hailed. He contacted the current owners of the mill, Michigan State University, as well as the Kellogg Company and Kellogg Foundation. His inquiries, however, were not fruitful, and the poldermolen remained at the Kellogg estate.

A visit to De Zwaan in the late 1960s by Joseph Lahaije, a Dutch immigrant then living in Indiana, would unexpectedly reveal another important piece of history about De Zwaan while it stood in Vinkel, something not even known by its former owner. As soon as Lahaije learned of De Zwaan's presence in Holland, he made a special trip to see the

*John Heuvel took over as De Zwaan's miller in 1968 and held the position through the 1990s.* City of Holland, Windmill Island Archives.

mill. As he stood in De Zwaan again for the first time in more than twenty-five years, he shared his remarkable story with a tour guide. In 1940, when he was twenty-one and working for the Dutch Resistance, he and another Dutch teenager had been sent on a mission to move a Jewish boy from one village to another so that he could remain in hiding and continue to work his way to safety. As they approached the village, they were warned by some boys in an outlying field that the town was crawling with Nazi soldiers. Lahaije and his partner realized that it would not be safe to attempt their mission that day and abandoned the plan. However, before they could turn back, they were spotted by a group of soldiers. The two young men took off running and continued as far as they could until they came upon De Zwaan. They crawled inside through a broken window and hurried up the ladders to the very top of the mill inside the cap. When they heard the sound of the soldiers in the mill, they flattened themselves on a beam and tried to breathe lightly despite their pounding hearts. Not finding the pair, the soldiers soon departed, but Lahaije suspected they might be lying in wait outside. He and his partner remained on the beam for hours until well into the night. Only then did they risk sneaking down to the first level and climbing back out the window. Still not convinced the soldiers were gone, they crawled on their bellies through the open field, before they got away to safety.

Four months later, while on another mission, Lahaije was captured by the Nazis and sent to a labor camp. He was released two years later in miserable physical condition. His sister nursed him back to health, and soon thereafter he returned to his work with the Dutch Resistance. His compassion and tenacity, as well as that of the myriad other Resistance workers, would save the lives of countless people during that agonizing and frightening time.

After the war, Lahaije, like so many other Dutch people facing trying economic times in The Netherlands, immigrated to America seeking new opportunities. Over the years, he made regular trips to Holland bringing family and friends to hear how De Zwaan had saved his life during the war. Even today, guides share Lahaije's special story with visitors.

Nelson Bosman stepped down in 1971 after ten years as mayor and he always recalled Windmill Island as one of his proudest legacies. During the years from the opening of the Island in 1965 to 1971, attendance had consistently averaged 112,000 visitors each year, a healthy showing, but significantly less than the consultant Frank Suggitt had estimated.

As the years passed, Willard Wichers and the Windmill Committee stayed in close contact with the Dutch Mill Society, a relationship that still endures today. Beginning in 1968, Wichers and Arie de Koning assisted the Mennonite Historical Society in Steinbach, Manitoba, Canada, which wanted to build a replica of a windmill that had been constructed there in 1877 by Peter Barkman, a Russian miller and millwright, for a community settled by Mennonite immi-

*Joseph Lahaije, whose life was saved when he hid from soldiers in De Zwaan at age 21, is seen here ten years after the ordeal. He was born in Kerkrade, and later lived in Heerlen. He died in 1999.* Photo courtesy Joann Lashbrook.

grants from the Ukraine. The mill had been sold by its original owner, A. S. Friesen, in 1879, then moved to another town and eventually torn down in 1920. In 1968, J. J. Reimer, the president of the Mennonite Historical Society, visited De Zwaan, and by 1970 had made plans to move forward with the project.

Diek Medendorp was hired to build the mill, which would be fabricated from many parts. The sixty-foot blades, the cap, and the fan tail, which is used to automatically turn the cap and blades into the wind, were built new in The Netherlands. The millstones, gears, and windshaft came from the 120-year-old windmill Sophia from the town of Tensbuettel in Germany.

In June 1972, Medendorp arrived in Steinbach for a five-month stay to build the mill on a site chosen by Arie de Koning at the Mennonite Village Museum. By early November that year, Medendorp had ground the first batch of flour and trained a local man, John Andres, who had worked with Medendorp during the construction, to be the first miller, just as he had trained Schrotenboer and Heuvel in Holland.

As Windmill Island continued to draw tourists, the city of Holland decided it wanted an antique Dutch carousel, and asked Diek Medendorp to help. Soon thereafter, Medendorp found the perfect

*Willard Wichers, Arie de Koning, and Diek Medendorp all played roles in helping erect a Dutch windmill at The Mennonite Village Museum in Steinbach, Manitoba, Canada.* Author's Collection.

carousel in Groningen, where he lived. The nine-meter carousel had been made by R. Ellinga from Vriescheloo in 1921, the second carousel he had built. The work on the organ and horses had been started by R. Meijer of Bellingwolde, but Ellinga took over the work and did the painting himself. In the beginning, the carousel (called a draaimolen in Dutch) was powered by a horse and lit with gas lamps. Ellinga quickly modernized it with an electric motor and lights in an effort to attract more customers. By 1938, he had sold the well-kept carousel to Hendrik de Boer, who then took the carousel to fairs

all over Groningen. De Boer died in January of 1964, and his children, who were not interested in continuing its operation, sold it to H. de Beer from Winschoten; he continued its operation at fairs for the next five years. When Medendorp began seeking a carousel in 1971, de Beer was willing to sell it to the city of Holland for $4,750.

In December of 1976, Medendorp returned to Holland for a three-week stay to replace the twenty-three-foot-long, sixteen-inch-square koningspil (main center shaft) in the windmill, which he had repaired in 1968. The new shaft was made of oak. Miller John Heuvel worked with him on the project, as the first miller Maynard Schroetenboer had done previously. While Medendorp was there, he also dressed the millstones to keep them sharp for grinding the grain.

De Zwaan was graced with another royal visit on June 26, 1982, when Queen Beatrix, the daughter of Prince Bernhard, made an impromptu stop during a brief visit to Holland. She climbed to the top of the mill that her father had dedicated.

In 1983, the city erected another building between the Zaandam houses and the concession building to use as a gift store, based upon another section of the Royal Orphanage in Buren, a one-story wing with stepped gables typical of traditional Dutch architecture. (Today the orphanage in Buren houses the Military Police Museum.)

By the twentieth year of operation, Windmill Island had drawn more than two million visitors under de Blecourt's management. The island continued to be self-sustaining, drawing well over 100,000 people each year and record crowds of over 122,000 people in 1972 and 1988. To celebrate the twenty-fifth anniversary on April 28, 1990, city of-

The "Draaimolen" at Windmill Island

ficials, community leaders, and friends of the windmill were invited to an open house with a special ceremony at the site, and the citizens of Holland were treated to a variety of entertainment including puppet shows, a sketching contest, free balloons, and music. A special anniversary painting of the windmill by local artist Gary Odmark was unveiled. That year, the entrance was redesigned, widening the road to three lanes, and a new ticket booth was built farther south.

The idea of building a Friesian farmhouse and barn was reconsidered at the encouragement of Fred Hekstra, a home builder in Byron Center, who hailed from a family of barn builders and thatchers, and had immigrated in 1953. In 1990, he made a trip to The Netherlands and visited the farmhouse from Midlum at the Openluchtmuseum in Arnhem. He ordered detailed blueprints of the structures and presented them to the Windmill Committee and the Holland City Council. City Manager Soren Wolff pursued getting an estimate for the construction, which was about $500,000. He said at a council meeting, "Once you see these plans, you can really get excited …. The timing for this is good, but we need to make sure that we keep going with this."

Responsible for the city budget, Wolff cautiously moved forward with the project, and by mid-1992 the city had saved $480,000. However, in the prior two years, visitation to the island had declined significantly and the operating costs had gone up, prompting the city council to delay the new construction project. Wolff reminded the council that Windmill Island had always been funded without taxpayer dollars and that city officials hoped to keep it that way. He added, "I think what we're saying is if we're going to spend $500,000, we've got to increase attendance." It was decided that an ad-hoc committee would be formed for the purpose of creating a final plan.

At that time, the city received pressure to restore De Vier Kolommen (The Four Columns), the barrel organ that had been given to Holland in 1947 by a committee of Amsterdam residents in recognition of Holland's support during the war.

The sixty-nine-key organ had been built in 1928 by Carl Frei in North Brabant, The Netherlands. It was proudly played during Tulip Time parades in the 1940s and 50s, and during the first season of Windmill Island in 1965, but had been kept in storage on the island ever since. In 1991, W. F. Snoerwang, chairman of the Circle of Friends of the Street Organs in The Netherlands, sent a letter to Holland officials, noting, "Several Dutch organ friends who visited Holland in the last few years have seen the organ in its deplorable state and have made photographs on which the damage clearly can be seen. Total destruction seems just a matter of time. Keeping this organ in Holland, Michigan, in the neglected state it is in now does not serve any purpose at all." The group wanted to buy back Four Columns, restore it, and play it on the streets of Amsterdam again.

Dutch-born Holland mayor Neal Berghoef noted in 1992 that he understood why the Dutch would want the ornate street organ back. "Four Columns street organ is a matter of both historical significance and emotion to the Dutch. I feel when they gave us this street organ, they gave us something they really loved," he said.

Although the city of Holland did not choose to sell back the organ, the criticism did help "sensitize city officials to the realization that something needed to be done with the organ," according to Ann Kiewel, the director of the Holland Historical Trust at the time. In 1993, the trust took charge of collecting private donations to restore the organ, which would cost as much as $40,000, hoping to have it completed by the 1994 Tulip Time Festival. De Blecourt began planning a small barn where it could be on display as a new attraction at Windmill Island.

The financial struggles were underscored by a $600,000 improvement bond taken several years earlier, which required the city to pay back $68,000 annually in addition to other normal expenses. On top of these looming financial burdens, attendance continued slipping, and in 1994 only 80,000 people visited the island. The increased admission cost may have been partly responsible. Then, in January 1995, during this very difficult time, Jaap de Blecourt, who had served as the island's manager for almost thirty years, announced his plans to retire before the start of the next season. Without a solid plan for the future, the city made no immediate plans to replace him.

Salvation seemed to appear at Tulip Time that year when two representatives of the Dutch company Forthuis, Bulder and Van Dijk visited Windmill Island and proposed a joint effort with the city, Tulip Time Inc., and the Holland Area Chamber of Commerce. The company offered to serve as a liaison between Holland and Dutch institutions that could bring authentic Dutch products to Holland and form trade links between local and Dutch businesses, erect authentic buildings from the northern provinces of The Netherlands on Windmill Island, and provide on-site historical interpretation. Ann Kiewel, who met with the group while on a trip to The Netherlands, told the city council that the company is "in the business of selling history." She noted, "I'm particularly struck with their desire for authenticity with what they want to do with Windmill Island. Their aim is to create sort of a living outdoor museum that has breathing, active people in it. This would be an opportunity to tell the story of the villages where many of our people came from."

*Prints of a beautiful painting of De Zwaan by Gary Odmark were sold at the twenty-fifth anniversary of the mill in Holland.* City of Holland, Windmill Island Archives.

The city council appointed a nine-person advisory board in September 1995 to help oversee the proposed project in hopes of improving attendance and the financial situation of Windmill Island. A three-person delegation was sent on a fact-finding mission to The Netherlands in October 1995 to pursue the Dutch company's plan to transform Windmill Island into a living historical village where people would live, work, and shop, similar to two historic villages that the company had developed in The Netherlands.

A tentative Holland/Netherlands partnership was announced in November 1995 with the expectation of breaking ground at Tulip Time the next year. This radical step to reinvigorate the island included developing a Dutch-themed neighborhood with homes, professional offices, and retail stores surrounding a church, a school, and De Zwaan. The plan also included a Dutch pavilion, which would be used as a visitor center and for the promotion of trade between Dutch and American companies, and the Friesian barn that had been discussed for years. City planner Phil Meyer, Greg Holcombe of the Riverview Group, and representatives from GMB Architects and Engineers served as key consultants along with staff of Forthuis, Bulder and Van Dijk, including Bert Bulder and architects Maarten Schmitt and Jan Does.

In February 1996, the city of Holland hired Dutchman Ad van den Akker as the new manager of Windmill Island. He came to the job with degrees and experience in business and marketing and had previously managed the operation at Nelis' Dutch Village in Holland from 1984 to 1987. Prior to accepting the position at Windmill Island, he and his wife, Karin, a graduate of Hope College, and their two children had been living in The Netherlands where he managed a laundry and linen rental service. Van den Akker felt that their return to Holland would

*The Four Columns barrel organ from Amsterdam was fully restored by 1997.* City of Holland, Windmill Island Archives.

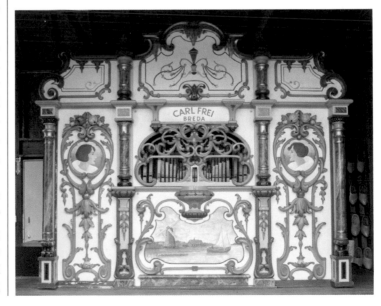

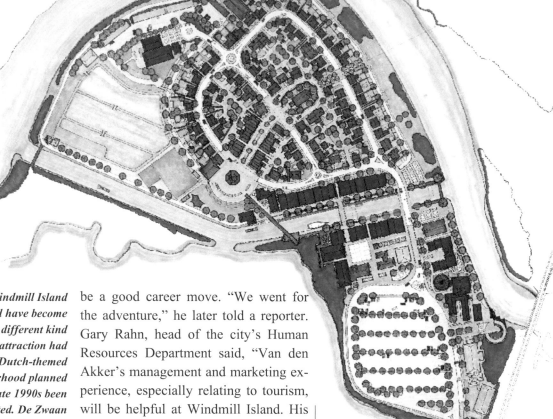

be a good career move. "We went for the adventure," he later told a reporter. Gary Rahn, head of the city's Human Resources Department said, "Van den Akker's management and marketing experience, especially relating to tourism, will be helpful at Windmill Island. His Dutch background and bilingual capabilities may also be an advantage as the city works to turn Windmill Island into a new neighborhood with nineteenth-century Dutch buildings."

Van den Akker's first Tulip Time at the island was both memorable and challenging when he had to handle a tragic accident that occurred at the windmill. On Saturday, May 11, 1996, Delwyn Ter Beek, a tree-trimmer by trade, who had been working for the previous twenty years on exterior maintenance and repairs on De Zwaan, fell thirty feet from the gallery of the mill and sustained severe head injuries that led to his death. While no one saw the fall, visitors had seen him pushing the windmill's blades, apparently trying to get them moving. The Michigan Occupational Safety and Health

Administration looked into the accident and decided not to issue any fines or citations in connection with the incident because, it determined, Ter Beek had been an independent contractor responsible for his own safety.

In regard to the safety on the mill, Curt Wright, the director of the Leisure and Cultural Services Department for the city of Holland, told reporters, "An accident can happen to even the most proficient man. We'll always be mindful [of Ter Beek's accident] and try to make sure that we stress ongoing safety."

On April 25, 1998, an oak tree and bronze plaque was dedicated at Windmill Island in Ter Beek's memory and in appreciation for his twenty years of service and dedication to De Zwaan.

The death of Del Ter Beek was a major loss for miller John Heuvel. The two had spent many years working together on the mill. Heuvel retired in 1999, though he made a commitment to assist the following season to keep the mill operational. Because of the uncertainty about the Dutch-themed neighborhood, the city did not commit to hiring a full-time miller. However, Ad van den Akker called upon Rob Zaagman, a second shift quality control specialist at Haworth, who had volunteered for waterway cleanup on the island through the local nonprofit Macatawa Greenway. Heuvel spent time with him teaching the milling trade and they were able to continue making flour.

In 2000, it became clear that De Zwaan's nearly 100-year-old blades would need to be replaced. Through Dutch contacts, van den Akker identified Lucas Verbij, a fourth-generation millwright from the firm Verbij b.v., located in Hoogmade, South Holland, The Netherlands, to do the work. The existing blades had been made by the firm Gebroeders Pot, located near Kinderdijk in The Netherlands, and installed on De Zwaan in 1902 when it was moved to its second location in Vinkel. The maker's plate and a section of the old metal sail stock were saved so that visitors could get a glimpse of the numerous bullet holes that it sustained during the war.

As the work on the blades commenced, van den Akker continued to assist with plans for the Dutch-themed neighborhood. The city would provide the infrastructure for the development, and the residential and retail owners would purchase lots and cover their own

*Rob Zaagman served as De Zwaan's miller in a volunteer capacity from 2001 to 2006 and continued to donate his time to beautify the island landscaping until 2014.* City of Holland, Windmill Island Archives.

construction costs. Real estate taxes would sustain the development and allow for the continued operation of De Zwaan as a tourist attraction.

Initially the project met with an enthusiastic response: Buyers placed deposits on all the lots, the city obtained several grants, and local developer Ted Bosgraaf agreed to develop and manage the commercial space as well as condominiums. However, rising estimates for infrastructure and a requirement by the Michigan Department of Environmental Quality to raise the island above the flood plain stalled the project. Attempts to revive it through the establishment of a nonprofit group, the Windmill Island Heritage Board, looked promising, but then Bosgraaf pulled out of the project.

Grand Rapids developer Paul Heule of Eenhoorn LLC, a native of The Netherlands and honorary consul of the Dutch Consulate in West Michigan, proposed becoming the developer of the community. Hopes were high among city officials and residents of Holland that the plan would save the island and De Zwaan.

# 6

# Maiden Miller

The plans to convert Windmill Island into a Dutch-themed neighborhood had been getting some press, and a friend of mine, who had heard of John Heuvel's retirement and knew that I had started looking for a job, suggested that I inquire about possible opportunities at the island. I had left my position as education director at the Holland Museum twenty-one months earlier to start a family, but had recently been considering a part-time position. In early 2002, I placed a call to Ad van den Akker. Not quite sure how to begin the conversation, I simply said, "I thought you might like to know that there is another miller in Holland."

"Oh?" he replied in his Dutch accent. "Is it your father or your husband?"

"No … it's me."

There was silence on the line for a few seconds as he must have been pondering my pronouncement. There were few millers and even fewer women millers, and I wondered if he would be open to discussing the trade with me. Much to my relief he replied, "I think we should talk."

We met in February at the island. I brought my resumé and my son Charlie, and van den Akker was very gracious. We talked about my background in living

*Alisa Crawford begins the grinding process in De Zwaan.* Photograph by Susan Andress.

history and open air museums, including my work at Colonial Williamsburg, Old Sturbridge Village, and Greenfield Village. He seemed interested in my experience, but did not offer me a job. The tug of an opportunity to work at a mill once more prompted me to make a follow-up call in March. Much to my delight, van den Akker invited me back, this time to tour the mill. As I walked in, the familiar smell of grain and flour I remembered from my youth made me feel nostalgic. I knew at that moment that I wanted to be a miller again. We climbed up to the milling floor where I met Rob Zaagman, who had been volunteering as miller.

"We're going to have you try to operate the brake," van den Akker said.

*Ad van den Akker has served as the manager of Windmill Island since 1996.* City of Holland, Windmill Island Archives.

I realized I was about to be tested. I had only previously operated a water-powered grist mill, and a windmill operates much differently and would require more strength. I hoped that my years of hauling sacks of grain prepared me for this. They escorted me out onto the gallery, and Zaagman demonstrated the process of starting and stopping the blades.

At that time, De Zwaan used a chain for the brake, and since it was still cold and damp in March, the brake chain was a little rusty and, on top of that, I didn't have any gloves. But I knew that if I couldn't manage it, I would not have a chance at this job. I grabbed hold of the chain, pulled down, and released the brake, and the blades began to revolve. Then I held tight to the chain and slowly released it until the blades came to a stop. "Okay," van den Akker said, encouragingly.

Then Zaagman asked me to do it again. And again. And again.

I must have passed the test, because days later van den Akker offered me a position, acknowledging that my milling

*For the first several years, Alisa Crawford focused on the sifting and packaging steps in the milling process at De Zwaan.* Photograph by Carolyn Stitch.

aptitude, as well as my programming, education, and interpretation experience at various museums, would come in handy. With the future of the Dutch-themed neighborhood still in flux, staff needed to be flexible, he pointed out.

On March 26, 2002, I reported for my first half-day at De Zwaan, taking over after Zaagman finished his work in the morning. As I walked the path to the mill that early afternoon, I had no idea that I was beginning a journey that would change the course of my life.

Although I had spent many years working at the water-powered Atlas Mill at Crossroads Village, a wind-powered mill operates quite differently. Initially Zaagman handled the grinding process, and I carried out the sifting and packaging. Together our efforts ensured that there would be plenty of flour to offer De Zwaan's visitors.

Looking back to my time at the Atlas Mill as a teen, I never imagined I would again work as a miller, but here I was doing just that. However, if I was ever going to grind grain, I would need more training. I had spent two years as an apprentice at the Atlas Mill before I could handle it alone, and because of the dynamics to harness the wind, I knew I would need at least twice that time to learn De Zwaan's operation.

Zaagman trained me when time allowed, but I also spent time on my own learning all I could. I located an English translation of the book *Molens* by the Dutch Mill Society's former president, Frederick Stokhuyzen, considered the "Bible" for Dutch windmills. I studied each page and the excellent illustrations and diagrams. Stokhuyzen described the role of the miller: "The trade requires devotion. This is to be met with in those who have been brought up to the trade and in the few outsiders who feel attracted to it, but their numbers are not great." I learned that there is a saying in The Netherlands about millers who have a love and appreciation for the trade: "being bit by the mill virus." I admit, I had been bit.

The course of Windmill Island and my working career changed in August 2002, just a few months after I was hired. After seven years of planning the Dutch-themed neighborhood, Holland mayor Al McGeehan and City Manager Soren Wolff announced that Holland and Paul Heule of Eenhoorn, LLC "were not able to put together a viable strategy" for the proposed village at Windmill Island. Deposits were returned to people who had purchased lots, and the future of Windmill Island and De Zwaan looked uncertain.

In the wake of losing that project, the city began making plans for changes that would keep Windmill Island operational. Only 53,000 people visited in 2002, 40 percent of them during Tulip Time. In an attempt to drive up attendance, the city council offered Holland residents free admission, but that did not help the budget. There were only 49,000 paying customers in 2003. In response, Ad van den Akker suggested opening up the island to weddings and other special events as a way to bring in more revenue. His plan would reinvigorate the island in ways the council had not previously imagined, and it also brought new responsibilities to my job. I was asked to get more involved in handling work in the office and helping with the various events.

In 2004, we began developing plans for a large tented pavilion, a fifty-by-ninety-foot permanent structure with a hard surface floor that could be used for wedding receptions and other gatherings. That year we also offered the first of what would be many special events. At Halloween, we invited the public to "The Haunting of Windmill Island," assisted by members of Hope College sororities and fraternities. We decorated the island so that visitors could have a thoroughly spooky experience.

The next year, 2005, marked the fortieth anniversary of De Zwaan in Holland, and we planned a series of events for the summer season. We held a Colonial Life event, a reunion of past staff, and debuted a documentary about the first forty years of Windmill Island's operation, produced by two Hope College seniors under the direction of Dr. David Schock. With the completion of the Celebration Pavilion that year, we hosted eleven weddings. The island also was used for the Kunst-markt (Art Fair) at Tulip Time as well as the Bier and Muziek Fest, Petal Pops, company picnics, Hope College Community Day, reunions, business lunches, and fundraisers. We renamed the Halloween event "Tales, Trails and Treats," based on the story of Sleepy Hollow, or in this case "Windmill Hollow." Young visitors could trick-or-treat at the shops and ride on the carousel decked out for Halloween. Others could board a horse-drawn wagon where they might catch a glimpse of the Headless Horseman and tour the haunted windmill. From there, they could follow a "scary" path through the woods which led them to the Celebration Pavilion for cider and donuts. The event was so successful we continued it the following year.

In 2006, we added a beautiful gazebo with a nice view of the drawbridge and De Zwaan to serve as a site for wedding ceremonies; that year we hosted twenty weddings. As a spin-off of the Colonial Life event, we introduced the Historic Dutch Trade Fair during the Tulip Time Festi-

*Wedding ceremonies are often held at the gazebo overlooking De Zwaan.* Photograph by Dan Johnson Photography.

val, inviting area third, fourth, and fifth graders. The fair brought together historic merchants and re-enactors, representing the seventeenth and eighteenth centuries and provided an opportunity to interpret the influence of the Dutch in shaping colonial America and creating a multi-cultural society. The hoopla of the fortieth anniversary, the weddings, and other events brought in additional revenue, and general visitation remained steady.

My career took a new turn in 2006 when I was able to accept an invitation by the Dutch Mill Society to come to The Netherlands and train on windmills to further my experience. The city of Holland had turned down a similar offer extended to Maynard Schrotenboer in 1966, but encouraged my opportunity forty years later. The offer to me resulted from a casual chat with a Dutchman, Mark Langerhorst, when he visited De

*The bridge is just one of many historic sites on Windmill Island that provide an excellent backdrop for weddings.* Photograph by Davyn Photography.

*The Celebration Pavilion can seat 300 people for wedding receptions.* Photograph by Dan Johnson Photography.

Zwaan in 2003. Langerhorst had enjoyed his visit and asked if there was anything he could do for me in The Netherlands. I asked if he could find out if there were any women millers there and if he could gather some information about a Dutch miller training program.

Just a few weeks later, he emailed me. Through the Dutch Mill Society, he had learned of three Dutch-certified women millers and had contact information for two of them: Aggie Fluitman, who operated a water-pumping mill in Alkmaar, and Josien de Vries, who worked on a grain mill in Wijk bij Duurstede. After I talked with them, both women offered to help arrange training for me in The Netherlands.

I received a grant from the Society for the Preservation of Old Mills in the United States, and the Dutch Mill Society, the Zaan Mill Society, and the millwright firm Verbij arranged opportunities for me

*The Celebration Pavilion serves as a space for wedding receptions and other events.* City of Holland, Windmill Island Archives.

Photograph by Dan Johnson Photography.

*Each year since 2006, school groups have visited Windmill Island during the Historic Dutch Trade Fair.* Photograph by Valerie van Heest.

*In 2005 and 2006 Windmill Island hosted a Halloween event at which the Headless Horseman made an appearance.* Photograph by Dan Irving.

to train in The Netherlands. I flew there in March 2006 to work on several grain mills, a paint mill, a paper mill, an oil mill, and water-pumping mills, including the mills run by Fluitman and de Vries, who serve in a volunteer capacity. I also visited the offices of the Dutch Mill Society and the workshops of Verbij.

During the end of a tiring day working with Aggie Fluitman on a water-pumping mill, she made a comment that would propel me even further in the trade. "There must be a way for you to go through the miller training program like I did," she said.

"I don't think so," I replied. "I am an American, it's a two-year program, and I have a young child."

She promised to inquire whether permission might be given to allow an American miller working on a Dutch windmill into the program.

The Guild of Millers and the Dutch Mill Society had never had a request from an overseas student. After much consideration, they decided to allow me into the program, however, I would need to accrue 150 hours training under Dutch-certified millers. Fluitman offered to come to Holland to help me begin my training for a month in May 2006. She taught me the technical Dutch mill words and we worked through the study books. My biggest stumbling block was that the program was in Dutch, so I pursued additional language study with a professor emeritus at Hope College, Dr. Phil Van Eyl, whose native tongue is Dutch. He and I worked together over the next year to prepare me to take the toelatingsexamen (proof exam), a requirement before taking the final exam.

That summer, I had the opportunity to train with Wouter Pfeiffer, a miller from The Netherlands whose wife was employed by the Dutch Mill Society. The couple interrupted their vacation in the United States so that he could work with me at De Zwaan.

I returned to The Netherlands in June 2007 to finish my required hours of training under Dutch-certified millers, attend the International Mill Society Symposium, and take the proof exam, which I passed. When I went back three months later for the final exam, I was delighted to have special guests present, including Dr. Phil Van Eyl, Arie de Koning, the director of the Dutch Mill Society Leo Endedijk, and several of the Dutch millers with whom I had trained. The exam was given at the grain mill De Zandhaas (The Sand Hare) in Santpoort, North Holland. When I passed the exam, I became the first Dutch-certified miller in the Americas.

Soon after my return to Holland, I was made a full-time employee of the city, both as De Zwaan's miller and as the event coordinator. That season the island hosted twenty-seven weddings and a number of other events, including a pirate island-themed Halloween celebration.

As part of my job, I speak about De Zwaan and milling to local organizations. During one program at Freedom Village, a retirement community that is De Zwaan's closest neighbor with views of the mill, I explained how most Dutch windmills have sails that can be hung from the blades to harness more power when the wind is light, though De Zwaan's had long ago deteriorated. After the presentation, residents Al Boers, Harold Gazan, and Dick Stafford offered to lead a fundraising campaign to raise money for sails, and by early 2008 they had over $8,000 in hand. The sails were made by a Dutch sailmaker, shipped to Holland, and installed with their necessary hardware in April by Gerard Kleijn, a millwright with the firm Verbij. Sporting its new sails, De Zwaan opened for the 2008 season as the main attraction of Windmill Island Gardens, renamed to attract horticultural enthusiasts as well as people interested in history.

No sooner had I become a full-time miller operating De Zwaan with its new sails than Aggie Fluitman suggested, "Now you need to go on for the professional level for grain millers."

Wouter Pfeiffer, a grain miller, requested permission on my behalf, and by the fall of 2008 I began the program with the assistance of Bert van der Voet, the secretary of the Ambachtelijk Korenmolenaars Gilde (Professional and Traditional Grain Millers Guild), who sent me two thick books in Dutch to study.

*Alisa Crawford passed her milling exam in The Netherlands in 2007 and became the first Dutch-certified miller in the Americas.* Photograph by Aggie Fluitman.

*In 2010, Windmill Island and De Zwaan were used for five days as a location to replicate* The Netherlands *when shooting the movie* **Return to the Hiding Place,** *which was released in 2013.*

*De Zwaan proudly displays the crest of the Professional Grain Millers Guild of The Netherlands signifying Alisa Crawford's membership in this elite organization.*

I returned to The Netherlands in April 2009 to sit for the qualifying exam, along with fifteen other grain millers—all men. All of us passed except two. In October I went back again for the next step: mandatory baking classes at the Vakschool in Wageningen. For the final requirement, van der Voet traveled to Holland later that month to assess my work on De Zwaan. He announced that I had passed the test and invited me to join the guild at a ceremony at Freedom Village witnessed by 250 people. I became the thirty-sixth member of the guild, and the only woman yet admitted. I was admitted at the journeyman level, and after ten years I can be reviewed for promotion to the master miller level.

Until then, I will focus on producing flour at De Zwaan, a process I have come to love. It is not always a one-person job, and I have been fortunate to have the assistance of several regular volunteers, including Dick Stafford at Freedom Village and Bryan Dozeman, among others.

The process starts when we bring fifty-pound sacks of grain to the mill in a motor vehicle. In the old days, farmers would have transported the grain by horse and cart, entering one set of doors and exiting the opposite set. To lift the heavy bags up five levels to the stone floor (fifth floor), we tie them, two at a time, to a rope that extends down through the grain elevator shaft from the stone floor to the first level. Using the power of the wind, which turns a friction gear on the spur wheel and winds the rope around the shaft like thread on a spool, we hoist the bags up to the stone floor and stack them near the millstones. We can also hoist them up manually using the "Y" wheel. We have to grind on the upper floor, closest to the power train, to maximize the wind's power.

The milling cannot begin until there is adequate wind, which is harnessed by rotating the cap and blades to face the prevailing wind direction. (Metal rollers ring the cap and allow it to rotate on a track.) From the gallery outside, I turn the capstan wheel to rotate the cap. If the wind is light, I can add sails to the blades to increase the wind's power. To do that I have to position the blades vertically one at a time, climb up, unfurl the sail, and tie it down with its ropes. Preparing to grind grain often requires as much as two hours of work.

Next I must climb the ladder to the dust floor (sixth floor), where I manually engage the stone gear with the spur wheel. This allows for the transfer of wind power from the spur wheel out to the stone gear, and then downward to turn the top millstone, known as the runner. We typically pour about 250 pounds of grain into the hopper, a wooden bin above the stones.

With the hopper loaded, the stone gear engaged, and the blades facing the wind, I go back out to the gallery to release the brake, allowing the blades to turn and power the top millstone, which is fifty-nine inches in diameter. The bottom stone, called the bedstone, remains stationary. The top stone turns at a rate of forty-five to sixty revolutions per minute. It is supported from underneath by a bearing and a system for raising or lowering the stone. The fineness of the flour is controlled by the amount of space between the two stones. For a fine grind, the stones may be separated by as little as the thickness of a sheet of paper; which requires the runner stone to be well balanced.

Each of the millstones has a series of grooves, called furrows. In De Zwaan as in other Dutch mills, the grooves run in a circular pattern. (In many American mills, the pattern is a series of straight furrows in graduated lengths.) The furrows serve three purposes: a cutting edge to crack open the grain, a path to get the ground grain to the edge of the stone, and an airspace to cool the grain, which gets warm from the friction. Once the mill is in operation, I release the grain from the hopper into the shoe, a wooden tray hanging above the millstone that feeds the grain into the eye of the stone at regular intervals. The release is controlled because the rotating shaft of the stone gear bumps the tongue of the shoe with every turn, thereby knocking more grain into the stone. If the wind picks up and the stone gear turns faster, more grain will be fed into the stone.

Traditional milling requires three variables that must work in harmony: the power of the wind, the feed of the grain, and the closeness of the millstones. The more that these can be controlled, the better the product. Since the wind is hard to control, the miller's reaction to the wind is most important. Milling requires employing all of the senses. I must watch the blades turn and count the revolutions to calculate the millstone's revolutions per minute. I have to listen to the sounds of the stones as they work together grinding the grain, and also to the sounds of the turning gears to make sure they are engaging properly. I must feel the texture of the

*De Zwaan's flour is sold in the shop on Windmill Island Gardens in a building that was constructed as a replica of a portion of the Royal Dutch Orphanage built in 1613 in Buren, Gelderland, The Netherlands. It is unclear why the replica was dated 1631.* Photograph by Greg Holcombe.

flour as it comes out to check its consistency and fineness. I must always keep alert for a burning smell, which can occur if the grain is not properly fed. When I bake with the finished product, I use my sense of taste to assess the quality of the flour. Traditional milling is an art learned through years of experience: watching, listening, feeling, smelling, and tasting.

With adequate wind power, using only one set of stones, the mill grinds an average of about 250 pounds of flour per hour. (De Zwaan has two sets of millstones but one is left open for educational purposes.) In a strong wind, I have ground as much as 600 pounds an hour.

Once the grain has been ground into flour, it descends through a chute to the storage floor (third floor) and is deposited in a stainless steel bin that can hold up to 4,400 pounds. Here the flour cools and ages for a short time. From there, the flour is released through a sliding door at the bottom of the bin to drop down another chute to the packaging floor (second floor), where it is sifted. The primary product produced at De Zwaan is a whole wheat flour, so during the sifting process only the largest pieces of the outer shell (the coarse bran) are removed. The fine- and medium-grades of bran are kept with the flour, ensuring that it is a healthful product filled with fiber and nutrients.

After sifting, the flour is packaged into two- or three-pound bags for retail sale or into fifty-pound bags for wholesale customers. Since we do not add preservatives, we freeze the smaller bags for forty-eight hours to prevent the natural oils from going rancid. After the freezing

*This view just below the cap in De Zwaan shows the rollers on which the cap spins and the large, wooden vertical brake wheel that meshes with the smaller wallower (spindle) gear.* Photograph by Bryan Dozeman.

*The millstones are typically not visible because a wooden vat surrounds them. The grain is fed down around the shaft through the eye of the top stone and ground between the stones. Flour comes out at the bottom inside the vat and is directed through a chute to the levels below.* Photograph by Bryan Dozeman.

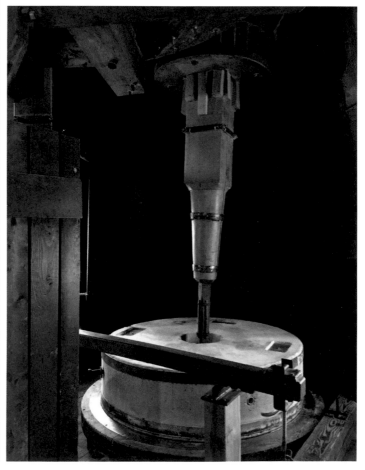

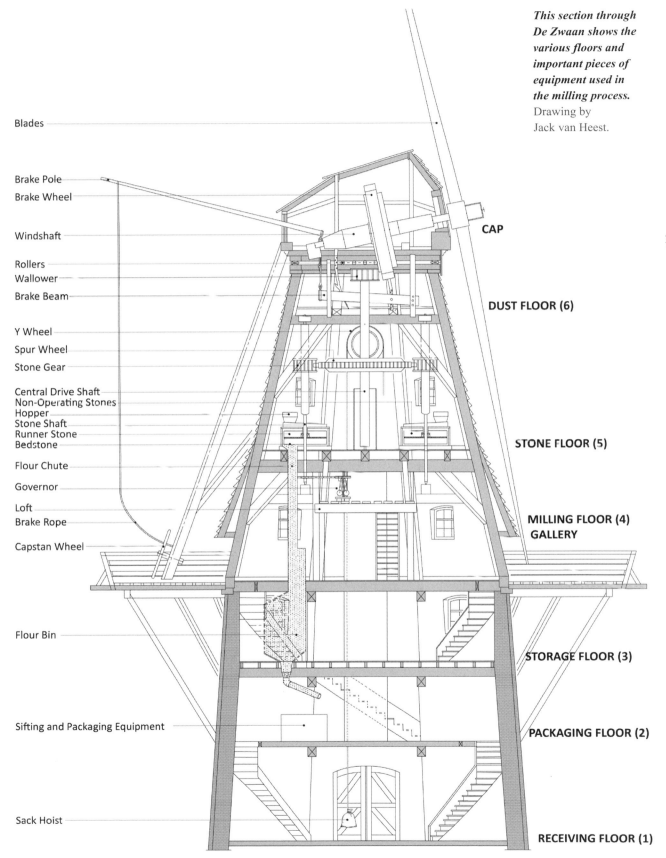

*This section through De Zwaan shows the various floors and important pieces of equipment used in the milling process.* Drawing by Jack van Heest.

Blades

Brake Pole
Brake Wheel

Windshaft

Rollers
Wallower
Brake Beam

Y Wheel
Spur Wheel
Stone Gear

Central Drive Shaft
Non-Operating Stones
Hopper
Stone Shaft
Runner Stone
Bedstone

Flour Chute

Governor

Loft
Brake Rope

Capstan Wheel

Flour Bin

Sifting and Packaging Equipment

Sack Hoist

CAP

DUST FLOOR (6)

STONE FLOOR (5)

MILLING FLOOR (4)
GALLERY

STORAGE FLOOR (3)

PACKAGING FLOOR (2)

RECEIVING FLOOR (1)

*When Diek Medendorp died on January 4, 2011, in Zuidlaren at age 89, miller Alisa Crawford set the blades in rouwstand (mourning position) shrouded in black sails, the traditional Dutch custom to signal the death of someone with close ties to the mill.* Photograph by Alisa Crawford.

Verbij determined that the entire system that allows the cap to rotate, inclusive of the water-damaged beam, needed replacement. The components included the beams that extend out from the cap connected to the long diagonal beams that end in the tail pole on the gallery, the capstan wheel, the rollers that turn on a metal track, and the brake. In addition, the lightning system needed updating to provide better grounding in the event of a storm, and the millstones required a new bearing, rebalancing, and additional adjustments so that the feed of the grain would be easier to control and allow for a better and more consistently ground product.

Under the leadership of Mayor Kurt Dykstra, City Manager Ryan Cotton, and Project Manager Jodi Syens, the city awarded the project to a local general contractor, Elzinga Volkers, which

cycle, the bags are moved to a cooler for longer-term storage or taken to the shop for sale.

In March 2012, the city again hired the millwright firm Verbij, this time to replace the worn upper gallery, and during that work millwright Gerard Kleijn discovered an extensive crack in a critical beam. To avoid further damage, he cut off the beam and locked the cap and blades in place so they could not turn until repairs were made. After much evaluation, the city chose to contract with the firm for a full restoration of the mill in order to return it to a safe, working condition.

In approaching windmill projects such as De Zwaan, Verbij tries to keep as much of the original mill as possible, helping ensure that it retains its characteristics as a Dutch mill. In the United States, this approach also has to be balanced with meeting building codes.

*Blue flags were set on De Zwaan to celebrate the birth of Alisa Crawford's son Alix.* Photograph by Bryan Dozeman.

worked under the direction of Gerard Kleijn from Verbij during the fall of 2013. The cap and the blades were removed by crane. Verbij built many of the pieces needed to restore the cap, some of the structural beams, and the turning system at their shop in The Netherlands and shipped them to Holland. Once the new system was installed, the entire mill was re-sided in cedar shingles and the cap received more than 4,000 shingles individually cut and hemmed from twenty-ounce sheet copper and secured in place with brass screws.

The two-and-a-half-month project cost $750,000, including a new bridge strong enough to provide access to the windmill side of the island for the heavy equipment needed for the restoration. The funds were raised through a combination of private donations and grants. People from greater West Michigan contributed monies, and the project received grants from the Michigan Economic Development Corporation, the Society for the Preservation of Old Mills, and the Prince Bernhard Cultural Fund in The Netherlands—a nice connection considering Prince Bernhard dedicated De Zwaan in 1965.

The generosity shown by the public was remarkable and gratifying, an affirmation that De Zwaan holds a special place in many hearts and that keeping it as a working windmill is a priority.

On Saturday, April 19, 2014, Holland officials celebrated the restoration of the windmill in a "Turning of the Blades" ceremony. It coincided with the start of the Run of the Mill 5K run organized by the Holland Youth Advisory Council, with the help of Gazelle Sports, to raise money for the maintenance of the windmill. At the moment the race began, the blades started turning again after standing still for two years. That year, the island attracted over 65,000 visitors, the highest number in fifteen years.

The Michigan Historic Preservation Network honored De Zwaan's restoration project with one of its 2014 Historic Preservation Awards. A statement from the organization called the project "the linchpin in the revitalization" of the island. The blades now move by the power of the wind to grind flour, as well as for the enjoyment of all, ensuring that an important historical and cultural artifact will live on.

*In 2013, contractors began to reinstall the restored cap of De Zwaan. The close-up photograph shows the many individual copper shingles that form the cap.* Photographs by Alisa Crawford.

# Revelations

Just as De Zwaan's future became secure, its past came into question. My quest to learn more about the history of De Zwaan began in 2005 after a Dutchman visited the mill while on vacation in Michigan. The quest was an undertaking that Willard Wichers acknowledged would be necessary when he wrote to the windmill committee in 1964, just after purchasing the mill: "It appears quite certain now that our mill has a long history…We will have to continue researching this history."

The visitor, Cees Knijnenberg, a former president of the Zaan Mill Society, met with Ad van den Akker, managing director of Windmill Island, who enjoyed conversing with him in his mother tongue. Ad later told me that Knijnenberg brought documents from the research of a Dutch mill scholar that included some surprising news: De Zwaan— "our" De Zwaan—did not hail from Krommenie in the Zaan District of North Holland, as the Dutch Mill Society had originally indicated in 1964.

While the documents were thought-provoking, they did not provide enough detail to prompt the alteration of everything that had already been recorded about De Zwaan. But as an historian, schooled to seek out the truth, I was certainly intrigued. I did not realize it at that moment, but I was starting to walk down a path that Willard Wichers had laid down for me decades earlier.

When I took my first trip to The Netherlands in March of 2006 for the purpose of training on Dutch windmills, I made it a point to visit the offices of the Dutch Mill Society in Amsterdam. The director of the society graciously arranged for me to meet Arie de Koning. De Koning was the society's former technical advisor and was heavily involved in finding and sending the mill to Holland, Michigan. It was a wonderful visit as de Koning fondly recalled his work helping Willard Wichers through the process in The Netherlands and his own visits to Holland on behalf of the project. He brought with him the scroll that had been given to him from Holland's city council in gratitude for his work. As he proudly showed it to me, I realized that this project had been a very memorable part of his life and career. I took the opportunity to thank him for the work he did on behalf of the city of Holland; his efforts played a key role in the mill as it stands today. While I had the burning question of the mill's origin in my mind, I did not find a proper opening to pursue it with de Koning that day. However, I learned that the society main-

*A detail of the painting,* **Houtkavels in het Wantij** *by Abraham van Strij, printed in the book* **Dordrecht 1650 - 1800** *by A. Molendijk, provides a vision of sawmills along the river in Dordrecht. Cut trees would be floated to the mills and sawed into lumber. One of these mills is perhaps De Zwaan that came to Holland.* Courtesy Piet Groot.

*Alisa Crawford met Arie de Koning, former technical advisor for the Dutch Mill Society, during a 2006 visit to The Netherlands.* Photograph by Leo Endedijk.

tains a vast archive of data about most of the mills built in The Netherlands. I visited the archives and with the help of Jan Klees, began to peruse the files. I vowed to spend time more time poring over the data on De Zwaan during a future visit.

I took up my mission when I returned to The Netherlands in June of 2007 to attend the symposium of the International Molinological Society (TIMS) and to continue my training on Dutch windmills. I was also there to take my toelatingsexamen (proof exam) for my Dutch miller's certification, which verified if I could be allowed to go on for the final exam. During the symposium, I asked a Dutch colleague from TIMS to see if he could arrange a meeting for me with Jan Diek Medendorp, the millwright responsible for reconstructing De Zwaan in Holland. It seemed that by meeting the people closest to the mill, I might come to learn more about it. My meeting with Medendorp was like a happy reunion. In the shadow of a mill that his great-grandfather had worked, we looked over old photos and postcards together,

each attempting to speak in the other's language. He reminisced about his time working in Holland, including getting his brand-new car stuck in the mud near the work site, and he shared some insights with me about the mill's condition when he first disassembled it, including that only five of the main upright achkant-stijlen (beams) could be reused. We talked of the mill's life in Vinkel, about the war and the heavy damage inflicted on the mill. As we discussed the mill's history, I recorded these words in my notes from my interview with him: "Krommenie or Dordrecht." Until then, I had never heard a reference to Dordrecht, a good-sized city in South Holland. I wondered why he mentioned it.

On a trip to The Netherlands in September 2007 for the purpose of taking the final exam for my Dutch miller's certification, I made time to return to the Dutch Mill Society to search through its archives. On September 20, I had the opportunity to look through the file on "our" De Zwaan, but I was disappointed to see that it was rather thin. Of course, the information contained in the file was all in Dutch, but by that time I could make out some of what it said. With the help of a TIMS colleague, Erik Stoop, who assists in the archives, I was able to learn some surprising things, not about the mill's origins as I had hoped, but about the arrangements through which the sale to Holland took place.

It will be recalled that Willard Wichers had simply been told that De Zwaan had been damaged during the war and its owner, Willem van Schayk, could not afford to restore it, which is how it became available to the city of Holland. The information in the file provided considerable additional information as well as an explanation of why Wichers purchased the mill from a millwright firm, not the miller, something that had come as very much of a surprise to Wichers on that June day in 1964.

De Zwaan and so many other structures had been badly damaged during the war and government aid was spread thin. Although van Schayk could keep grinding for animal feed after the war using a hammer mill powered by an engine, the mill structure was breaking down around it. In 1945, he began looking into the available government subsidies. But as with everything damaged during the war, help was not immediately forthcoming. As early as 1953, he reached out to the Dutch Mill Society and was put in touch with Arie de Koning. In August that year, the society sent M.C. van Aspert, an architect specializing in mill restoration, who provided an estimate for restoration of De Zwaan. He included repairing and recovering the body of the mill and the cap, repairing of the lattice framework on the blades, and fabricating two new sails so that the mill could turn by wind power again. He also included interior work such as replacing and repairing some beams, a new stone gear, repairing the stone floor, and addressing the wear on the two sets of millstones. The work would cost 3,279 guilders.

In late August 1953, van Schayk moved to the neighboring community of Geffen. He wrote to de Koning, worried that his relocation away from Vinkel, Nuland, where the mill stood might jeopardize his receipt of government funding. De Zwaan stood at the boundary between five municipalities, and with the miller living in a different municipality than the mill, government support would be more difficult to obtain.

Two years passed and no government subsidy materialized. The millwright firm Gebroeders Adriaens prepared an updated estimate for the restoration in June 1955. The firm divided its estimate into two parts: 4,950 guilders for repairs of damage incurred in the war, and 6,660 guilders for needed upgrades, a total of 11,610 guilders. However, government funding was not forthcoming and the mill continued to deteriorate. By 1956, Gebroeders Adriaens raised its restoration quote to 14,310 guilders.

In a continued effort to seek financial assistance on behalf of van Schayk, Gebroeders Adriaens submitted an estimate to Anton Bicker Caarten, a director at the Ministry of Cultural Heritage. By then, the firm had increased its total request for assistance by another 2,100 guilders to recover the cap and some other small repairs on the mill that van Schayk had already done. Gebroeders Adriaens proposed that the ministry pay 60 percent, indicating that van Schayk was ready to contribute 20 percent, the province should contribute 10 percent, and the local communities that would benefit from the windmill being in

*In 2007, Alisa Crawford met Diek Medendorp, the millwright who reassembled De Zwaan in 1964 and 1965.* Photograph by Erik Stoop.

operable condition should contribute the remaining 10 percent.

Finally, on August 14, 1957, Arie de Koning informed Gebroeders Adriaens that the government had agreed to fund not just 60 percent, but 65 percent of the restoration cost. However, the mill's location in one community, bordering four others, with the miller living away from the mill, complicated the efforts to get community support for a portion of the restoration. Without community funding, van Schayk could not proceed with the work.

In 1961, a concerned neighbor wrote the Dutch Mill Society reporting that nothing had been done and that it was now "regenen binnen & bouten" (raining inside and outside), in De Zwaan. By August of that year, the restoration cost had risen to 19,467 guilders. In November 1962, the Ministry of Education, Arts and Sciences advised van Schayk that he must begin the work immediately or lose the government subsidy. Even then, the local communities were not forthcoming with funds. This caused a great deal of frustration and disappointment for many individuals in Vinkel, but particularly for van Schayk. With no other options, he sold the mill to Gebroeders Adriaens in May of 1964 for 3,500 guilders. Gebroeders Adriaens likely bought it on speculation. It could dismantle the mill for parts, a common practice for aged mills, or perhaps sell it to the Americans who were seeking a mill, a fact the firm would have known through its association with Arie de Koning.

De Koning and the Dutch Mill Society must have considered that sending De Zwaan to Holland, Michigan, was certainly better than having it lost forever. This sequence of events is what brought Gebroeders Adriaens into the picture, not as a millwright, but as a broker.

Although Wichers had done his best to seek out a windmill for the lowest possible cost, hoping to arrange that through a direct sale from a miller to the city of Holland, it would have been unlikely that a miller would have had the connections to make such an arrangement. Considering the great effort that Gebroeders Adriaens had expended over the years providing restoration quotes and working with the government to seek funding to restore De Zwaan, it is understandable that the firm sought compensation in some way. In this case, Gebroeders Adriaens made about 4,500 guilders for its efforts, the difference between what it paid van Schayk for the mill and what it charged Holland.

This information certainly filled in some holes, but it did not bring me closer to understanding whether or not De Zwaan hailed from Krommenie. A book in the archive's library caught my attention: *Duizend Zaanse Molens* (1,000 Zaan Mills) by Pieter Boorsma, 1958. I paged through and found a section about a mill named De Zwaan in Krommenie. Able to read "milling Dutch," I immediately recognized two interesting facts about that mill. Its wingspan was 22 meters (72 feet), and it had been broken down in 1887. Suddenly I realized that our mill could not possibly have been De Zwaan that hailed from Krommenie. Its wingspan was considerably larger at 25.5 meters (80 feet), and De Zwaan had been moved to Vinkel in 1884, three years before the Krommenie windmill had been taken down. If our De Zwaan did not hail from Krommenie, then I wondered, *where did it truly come from?*

During that same trip, I received a phone call on Sunday morning, September 23, from mill historian Piet Groot. A colleague and I were headed to the Zuider-

*A photograph of the windmill called De Zwaan in Krommenie was recently found. Research has proven that windmill was not the one relocated to Vinkel and later Holland, Michigan.*
F. Role Collection from molendatabase.org.

Zee Museum in Enkhuizen that day, but the phone call seemed important, so I took time for it. He began the conversation by saying, "The history is not as you have been told," explaining that De Zwaan did not come from Krommenie in the Zaan District. This offered corroboration of what I had myself concluded just three days earlier. At that moment the reality of that fact washed over me and I struggled to accept that everything I had believed about the mill's origin simply was not true. I felt shocked, as if I had just been told I was adopted and had no idea who my birth parents were. After that phone call, I was even more determined to find out where the mill actually came from. Groot and I agreed to stay in contact, and he offered to continue his research.

By that time in my milling career, I had made a number of contacts within the small contingent of windmill historians in The Netherlands, and I began asking more and more questions of my Dutch colleagues. Near this time, I became aware of an online database www.molendatabase.org established for mill historians in 2001 by Jan van der Molen (certainly an appropriate name for a mill historian); it contains information on most of the 9,000 windmills that once existed in The Netherlands. When I first explored the database, I noted that

mill historian J. S. Bakker had posted his conclusion that Holland's De Zwaan did not hail from Krommenie. In addition to the issues with the blade length and date disassembled, he added that hemp mills simply never had blades that exceeded 22 meters, still further evidence refuting Krommenie as De Zwaan's birthplace.

In March 2008, Piet Groot's research would eventually point to De Zwaan's true provenance. He learned from van Schayk family oral history that *their* De Zwaan (therefore *our* De Zwaan) had come from the city of Dordrecht in South Holland, the same town mentioned by Medendorp. Groot searched through the mill database and found two windmills named De Zwaan in Dordrecht; both had been sawmills. De Zwaan (a) had burned several times and been rebuilt, but was still operating in Dordrecht in 1884 when De Zwaan was erected in Vinkel; therefore that mill (a) could not have been the one moved to Vinkel. Groot, along with another mill historian, Ton Meesters, noticed with great interest that De Zwaan (b) had been built in 1833 and was converted

*A detail of the map on page 57 shows the proximity of Dordrecht, where sawmill De Zwaan (b) operated from 1833 to 1884, to Vinkel, where the reconstituted mill stood from 1884 to 1964. In Vinkel, De Zwaan became a wind-powered grain mill using the body, cap, and blades from its sawmill forerunner, along with additional equipment from the Nooitgedacht grain mill in nearby Den Bosch.*

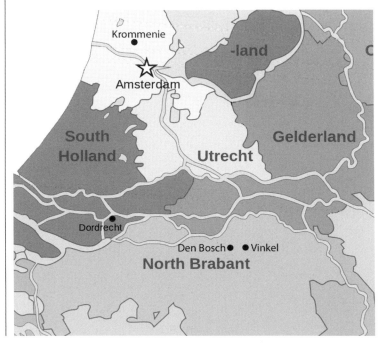

*This photograph shows the steam-operated sawmill De Zwaan as it stood in Dordrecht, circa 1900. When the mill was converted from wind power to steam power in 1884, it is believed that its body, cap, and blades were relocated to Vinkel and then, eighty years later, to Holland, Michigan. The sawmill continued to operate in Dordrecht until the 1960s, when it was demolished. When the photograph is enlarged, the name De Zwaan is visible near the peak of the largest building.* Courtesy of Piet Groot.

to steam in 1884. At that point, its eight-sided body, cap, and blades would have become superfluous. He concluded that the body of De Zwaan (b) had been purchased for relocation to Vinkel.

I plotted the location in Dordrecht where Groot told me that De Zwaan (b) had been built and realized that it would have been very convenient to put the mill on a boat and transport it via the Maas River and then a canal directly to Vinkel. In hindsight, it makes no sense that the miller in Vinkel would have purchased a mill body from as far away as Krommenie in North Holland. Transportation via water would have been long and circuitous, resulting in an expense exceeding the value of a second-hand mill.

The database provided a brief history of De Zwaan (b), which we now believe is *our* De Zwaan. A man called Hendrik den Turk originally built that windmill in Dordrecht in 1833. He operated it until 1859 when business slowed and it had to be sold at auction. Arie Driesse van de Weg then purchased the mill and passed it down to several generations in his family. After the windmill was converted to steam in 1884, it could continue to operate without its body and

blades. Those parts would have become available to use in building the windmill in Vinkel. The Dordrecht sawmill De Zwaan remained operational until the 1960s. In 1969 when the river was widened, the aged sawmill was demolished.

As Groot and the network of Dutch mill experts pondered this new realization, one of them was able to shed more light on De Zwaan's true origins. Ironically, the man with the answer was Nico Jurgens, who as an ailing teen had persuaded his father to take him to Vinkel in 1964 to photograph De Zwaan before it was disassembled. Jurgens, now a seasoned mill historian, agreed with Groot that De Zwaan likely hailed from Dordrecht. Supporting that conclusion, he knew that De Zwaan's windshaft had been made by the iron foundry Feyenoord and dated sometime before 1842 when the company began adding maker's marks. Feyenoord is located near Rotterdam, only a few miles from Dordrecht, making it more likely that it would have supplied windshafts for mills in that region, not as far north as Krommenie. Interestingly, Nico Jurgens also noted that the English (metal) rollers on De Zwaan's cap are tapered, an unusual type only seen in one other mill in Rotterdam.

*Windmill experts can tell just from looking at the star design on the outer end of the windshaft (which secures the two blades outside the cap) that it was made by the iron foundry Feyenoord, located near Dordrecht. Since there is no maker's mark on the shaft, experts know that it was manufactured before 1842, the year when the foundry began adding its mark.* Photograph by Alisa Crawford.

*This two-inch high makers mark, (upper right) is found on the staakijzer (metal shaft below the stone gear seen at right penetrating the opening in the top millstone). The mark indicates that it was made by J.V. Kuppeveld from Uden who was a well-known blacksmith in the early nineteenth century in the Den Bosch area.* Photographs by Bryan Dozeman.

He also explored how the sawmill De Zwaan would have been converted to a grain mill. H. F. de Vocht would have had to acquire millstones and other related grain milling equipment in order to convert the sawmill to a grain mill. Searching through the database of some 9,000 windmills, Jurgens discovered only one realistic candidate: a grain mill called Nooitgedacht (Never Thought) that had been built in 1800 and dismantled for parts in 1883. That mill once stood in 's-Hertogenbosch (often called Den Bosch), located a mere ten miles via canal from Vinkel. Transportation of the heavy parts, including the blue stones, (which are, incidentally, now on display in Holland outside De Zwaan) would have been convenient and economical for H.F. de Vocht. In addition, the staakijzer (metal shaft below the stone gear) bears the maker's mark from a blacksmith in Uden, which is near Den Bosch. Everything was beginning to add up.

Jurgens explored one more detail. He knew that when Medendorp disassembled De Zwaan in 1964, he found the spur wheel and stone gears, which together turn the millstones, to be in unusable condition. Knowing that Medendorp often drew from his vast collection of mill parts, Jurgens concluded that the replacement parts came from the much newer 1897-built Molen van Jonker grain mill that Medendorp had erected in Aruba in 1961. In its new incarnation as a restaurant, the mill would not have needed those parts.

Another phone call with Piet Groot in December 2014 convinced me that De Zwaan had lived a former life as a sawmill. Medendorp, whom Groot had met in the late 1970s, told him that when he broke down the mill, remains were still visible of its use as a sawmill. He had also noticed that a sawblade had been used in repairing some of the cross braces. These observations by an experienced millwright added a lot of weight to the sawmill theory.

Just when I thought I had learned everything possible about De Zwaan, there came a new twist. A former colleague from the Holland Museum, Joel Lefever, suggested I look through Willard Wichers' files at the Holland Museum Archives where he recalled seeing some correspondence disputing the mill's history. I told him that I had already thoroughly combed through three boxes labeled "Wichers' windmill files" and found nothing of that sort. Lefever pointed me to boxes that he recalled had never been catalogued. During my next visit to the archives, I learned that there were, in fact, over *eighty* boxes of Wichers' documents that had never been processed. Taking a deep breath, I resolved to go through each and every one, starting in the logical place: the upper left-hand corner of a wall of stacked boxes. Much to my surprise (and relief) the first box was loaded with manila folders all bearing the names of people and

subjects familiar to me—another box of windmill documents! After hours poring through original letters sent and received by Wichers, I found several documents that confirmed—in writing—what had taken me and the mill historians years to ferret out independently.

Less than two weeks after the mill's dedication in April 1965, someone in The Netherlands sent Wichers an article that had just appeared in the Amsterdam newspaper *Trouw* entitled, "Mill in Michigan is not from Zaan." It was clear from the article that Wichers' request to the government officials of the Zaan District for a bottle of water from the Zaan River for use in De Zwaan's dedication had prompted local mill authorities to investigate *their* De Zwaan. They realized that because *their* De Zwaan was taken down in 1887, it could not possibly have been the same mill erected in Vinkel in 1884, three years earlier.

That article was clearly upsetting to Wichers, who had just dedicated De Zwaan with much fanfare about its early history in the Zaan District. In fact, the map given to Holland by Prince Bernhard showing the mill's location in Krommenie and the bottle of water from the Zaan River were on public display in the post house. Wichers turned to Frederick Stokhuyzen, the president of the Dutch Mill Society, asking him to investigate the mill's history more thoroughly and provide a written statement about its history. In September 1965, Stokhuyzen forwarded a document from the Ministry of Foreign Affairs that confirmed, much to Wichers' relief, De Zwaan had indeed been built in Krommenie in 1761. However, six months later, Wichers received another letter from Stokhuyzen, dated March 14, 1966, that refuted the prior information, and showed how seriously the Dutch Mill Society had taken Wichers' charge to research De Zwaan's history. It began, "I can give you the answer on the subject of De Zwaan, though it can't be satisfying to either of us."

Stokhuyzen reported that after many discussions between de Koning, Medendorp, and historians Evert Smit, de Kramer, and Bakker, they could not find any proof that De Zwaan in Vinkel hailed from the Zaan District. All they could report was that the body came from one place and the grain milling equipment from another.

Willard Wichers' April 12 response to this new "surprising information," as he called it, is uncharacteristic of a man for whom the collection and interpretation of history was so important. However, it is completely understandable that he would try to protect the people involved. "We are caught somewhat in a trap of our own publicity," Wichers explained, referring to all public promotion about Holland's 200-year-old mill from the Zaan District. "It may be more prudent to submit this new evidence at a later date when the announcement would be less devastating… so as not to embarrass those associated with the earlier facts."

Stokhuyzen agreed, replying, "Best that the question can rest now and be open for the future."

As it turned out, fifty years would pass before that information would come to light while I was doing research for this book. I feel certain that Willard Wichers would be glad to know that De Zwaan's provenance has been determined—and shared—and that all these years later, the news is not "devastating," or "embarrassing," but in fact quite interesting.

It is clear that De Zwaan does not have a "purebred pedigree" dating to 1761 as once believed. It is, according to the best conclusion by mill his-torians today, a hybrid windmill fabricated most likely from the body of an 1833-built sawmill with the equipment from two grain mills built in 1800 and 1897. However, that lineage is what makes De Zwaan unequivocally *authentic*. Most windmills standing today have been modified and updated significantly. Kellogg's windmill near Battle Creek was erected with the parts from two different windmills. Even the windmill at the world-famous Keukenhof Gardens at Lisse is a hybrid of several windmills. Windmills were and continue to be working machines. When they break, they are repaired. When the parts wear out, they are replaced. When they become outmoded, they are repurposed.

De Zwaan is not the only authentic Dutch windmill in the United States and it may be considerably "younger" than the city of Holland was led to believe. However, an observation made by Gerard Kleijn of the firm Verbij, which restored De Zwaan in 2013, clouds that simple conclusion. "The achtkantstijlen (the eight-sided beams that form the mill body's structure) along with the boven-tafelelement (circular piece of wood at the top that joins the beams) and the type of wood that they are made from," he told me, "is the type often seen on mills manufactured in the eighteenth century."

The possibility exists that Hendrik den Turk, who built De Zwaan in Dordrecht in 1833, acquired a second-hand mill in what is the typical Dutch fashion for economy. And so, the mystery of De Zwaan's precise age will probably always linger.

Back in the 1960s, Willard Wichers and the windmill committee wanted a mill with a history and that is certainly what the city of Holland got. The history is just a bit different than originally believed.

# A Replica Mill For Vinkel

For the people of Vinkel, North Brabant, The Netherlands, De Zwaan's history before it was erected there in 1884 was of little consequence. In the eighty years it stood in the village of Vinkel, however, it became a beloved edifice. De Zwaan served as the center of the small community as most mills in agriculture societies have done since the beginning of communal living. Around the world, communities formed around a mill, whether its purpose was to grind grain, saw wood, make paper, press oil, or any of several other uses. Since food was among the most important requirements for survival, there was a natural dependence on grain mills. When farmers brought their grain to be ground, they had to wait for the milling to be completed; consequently, the mills typically became a gathering place where news and information were exchanged and friendships established. In its eight decades in Vinkel, De Zwaan had been all that and more.

On a fall day in 2010, I learned firsthand how important De Zwaan had been for Vinkel. My phone rang one early morning as my son and I were busy getting ready for school and work. I recog-

*De Zwaan served as a backdrop for weddings long before it was moved to Holland. Nel, daughter of De Zwaan's miller Willem van Schayk, posed for a wedding photo in the early 1960s.* Courtesy of Stichting de Vinkelse Molen.

nized that it was an international call, so I took time to answer. "Hello?" I said.

"Are you the molenaar van De Zwaan?" a man asked in half English, half Dutch.

"Ja," I responded, launching into Dutch. "Ik ben de molenaar."

His next words pierced me like a sword: "We vant our mill back!"

I was stunned and not sure how to respond, but he continued talking. He introduced himself as Ebert van Wanrooij, from a family that has lived in Vinkel for generations. He asked me how many bezoekers (visitors) De Zwaan receives a year, and I told him the number was typically over 55,000. "Then with 55,000 bezoekers, you probably don't want to give the mill back," he said dejectedly.

"Nee," I responded.

"Then I guess we have no other choice but to rebuild it," he announced, to my surprise.

After that phone call, my son and I scrambled out the door. As I drove my car, I felt numb, trying to absorb the content of the phone call and the exchange I just had with this Dutchman from Vinkel. I realized that something I loved so dearly was wanted desperately by someone else. After I got over the shock of the phone call, I started to think more about what the departure of the mill to America in 1964 must have meant to the people of Vinkel.

I recalled how Nico Jurgens told me he had begged his father to take him to see the mill before it was shipped across the ocean. I remembered that Jan Adriaens, of the millwright firm Gebroeders Adriaens, had told Willard Wichers that there was great pressure on him from the locals not to sell the mill. I realized that when the provincial authorities agreed to waive the six-month waiting period and allowed De Zwaan to be disassembled immediately, they took away any opportunity for the community to formally protest. I also thought about how the mayor of Nuland canceled the celebration over the sale when he learned the sadness of the community. Only then did I start to see things from the perspective of the Dutch.

Through my milling contacts in The Netherlands, I began to ask about Ebert van Wanrooij and his plans to rebuild the mill. I learned that although van Wanrooij was born after De Zwaan left, he grew up hearing stories from his parents of how the Americans "took" their mill. There was a whole generation of people in Vinkel, I found out, who had heard similar stories and felt that their community was missing something. Van Wanrooij began leading an effort to build a working replica of De Zwaan in Vinkel. He and a number of other individuals had formed the non-profit Stichting de Vinkelse Molen (Organization of the Vinkel Mill) hoping that a windmill would serve the same purpose as De Zwaan has served in Holland for fifty years: an historic attraction and icon for the community. Vinkel had about 1,000

residents when De Zwaan was taken down in 1964, and now the community had only grown to about 2,400. A windmill could serve as an economic stimulus there as it has for Holland.

To realize their dream, members of the organization knew that it would take a large sum of money. The volunteers began several fundraising programs. In 2010 they competed in a fundraising contest called the Dorpen Derby held among different towns to garner the highest number of votes for certain projects. As a semi-finalist, Stichting de Vinkelse Molen was given a monetary award toward the project. In addition in 2011 they opened the "Kringloopwinkel," a second-hand thrift store that provides another source of funds toward their goal.

I learned more about the efforts of

*The Stichting de Vinkelse Molen operates a store, the proceeds of which go toward the windmill fund.* Courtesy of Stichting de Vinkelse Molen.

the Stichting de Vinkelse Molen when two members of the organization, Rianne van der Biezen and her husband, Tonnie, visited De Zwaan during the summer of 2014. We had a chance to talk and exchanged gifts. She shared that the board of directors had just begun developing plans for a groundbreaking, set for August that year, to generate more support and additional necessary funds for the project; they wished to make sure that I would be invited so that I could say a few words about De Zwaan. However, the untimely death of one of their board members, Tonny van der Lee, delayed that event. His passing at just fifty-two years old was a tremendous shock and painful loss for his family and the community of Vinkel. Grieved for his family, especially his children, I sent a card from Holland with a photo of De Zwaan set in the mourning position, draped in black sails.

Knowing van der Lee would have wanted the organization to go forward with the project, the committee rescheduled the groundbreaking ceremony for November 23, and I arranged for my flight so I could be there to represent both De Zwaan and the city of Holland at this important ceremony. The committee also invited the five grown children of the last Vinkel miller, Willem van Schayk. I had met one of his daughters, Johanna (Ans) Schmidt van Schayk, when she made a visit to De Zwaan in July of 2007, and I looked forward to seeing her again.

Rianne van der Biezen picked me up at the Schiphol Airport in Amsterdam and drove me to Vinkel. It was a momentous occasion for me to finally see the little town from which De Zwaan hailed. On the day of the groundbreaking ceremony, Ebert van Wanrooij took me to the new church that had replaced the previous structure. In the church cemetery, I was reunited with

Ans Schmidt van Schayk and her husband. We stood at the grave of her parents, Willem and Bertha van Schayk, and talked about them and their beloved mill.

We then joined a group of people at the spot where De Zwaan once stood. Ans' three sisters and brother began to arrive one by one, until all of them were together again. A local news station interviewed the siblings, and I enjoyed hearing their memories about the mill when it was in operation.

After the interviews, the van Schayk family members and I were transported by a horse-drawn tram to a local restaurant for lunch. I sat next to Ans and had a chance to learn more about her family. Ans explained that her mother had given birth to seven children, but two had

*Tonny van der Lee served as a leading member of the Stichting de Vinkelse Molen before his untimely death.* Courtesy of Stichting de Vinkelse Molen.

*The Stichting de Vinkelse Molen unveiled in November 2014 a billboard announcing the project to rebuild De Zwaan.* Courtesy of Stichting de Vinkelse Molen.

died tragically. After the first daughter, Nel, was born, her mother gave birth to a boy, Jan. When he was four years old, he wandered into the path of De Zwaan's turning blades and was struck in the head. He was badly hurt, and because the area was so rural, his parents were unable to get needed medical help. The little boy survived for a couple of days, but died from his injury. Bertha soon gave birth to another daughter, Trees, followed by a boy they named Jan after their first son. Sadly, he only lived one day, so he is remembered as "Kleine Jan" (Little Jan). Johanna (Ans) was born next, named as the feminine version of Jan, after the two boys who died before she was born. Sister Maria (Mieke) and brother Piet followed. All the children grew up around De Zwaan.

After the lunch, the Friesian horses pulled our tram to the place where the local mayor unveiled a billboard promoting the mill project. Next we gathered at the banquet hall Dorstvlegel, where Ebert van Wanrooij, the man from whom I had first learned about the project, presented an update on the fundraising efforts.

From there, we were taken to the place where the mill will be rebuilt in Vinkeleskade South. While the organization would have liked to rebuild on the original site, the area is now too congested to provide adequate wind. The ceremony was presided over by Ebert van Wanrooij representing the Stichting Vinkelse Molen; Roel Augustijn, the mayor of Vinkel; and Lambert van Nistelrooij, a Netherlands member of the European Parliament who was born in Nuland. I watched as van Wanrooij selected two specific people, representing De Zwaan's past and future, to dig up a patch of ground. First he invited Nel, the oldest of the van Schayk siblings, followed by a little red-haired boy, the grandson of a committee member. The child was so eager to take part that he didn't want to stop digging. I was moved by all the smiles that day and thought about how different it was from June 1964 when sadness spread through the community as De Zwaan came down piece by piece.

After the ceremony, we returned to the banquet hall for a time of celebration and speeches. When I was introduced and asked to speak, I offered up, in Dutch, the same sentiment that Holland's mayor Nelson Bosman had shared fifty years earlier in a letter to the Reverend Jan Verkuylen, who had grown up near Vinkel and was upset by De Zwaan's move: "We can sympathize with the regret felt by the good people of Vinkel who have lost their mill and trust that in time, they will feel a close bond with the people of Holland, Michigan, who will share with them their affection for De Zwaan."

I concluded my talk by saying that "De Zwaan is onze molen" (De Zwaan is our mill), motioning to everyone. Then I presented a small piece of De Zwaan's original blade, salvaged after a recent renovation, as a gift to the Stichting de Vinkelse Molen and the van Schayk fam-

ily so they would always have a piece of De Zwaan from when it was in Vinkel.

After the ceremony, I had a chance to talk with a number of people to get a better understanding of why they want to rebuild De Zwaan. One of the committee members said that "the mill was a part of Vinkel and our history, and our history is very important to us." Another resident explained that "when the mill was taken down and sent to America, it was like the heart of the community had just been ripped out." I also met Hans Kappen, who has received the training to be the first miller of the new mill in Vinkel.

I could hear the determination to rebuild De Zwaan in their voices and see it in their eyes. They assured me that they are not resentful nor do they harbor ill will toward Holland, Michigan, but are instead investing their efforts in the new mill. We spoke of ways to work together so that they can realize their goal.

As I reflected on my participation in the groundbreaking fifty years after De Zwaan was disassembled, it struck me how prophetic Mayor Bosman's words had been in 1964 and how fortunate that I could deliver them in a way that helped solidify the bond between communities. I felt that I was completing the work that William Wichers, Mayor Bosman, and the other members of Project Windmill had started, and helping to heal the wound that had been created when De Zwaan was shipped to America.

# Fifty-Year Perspective

More than fifty years have passed since De Zwaan alighted in its new home in Holland, Michigan. In that time, the mill has been cared for by the city and a succession of its millers. As of late, it has been fully restored and is again operational.

Although millions of people have visited De Zwaan during the fifty years it has lived in America, to the community of Holland, Michigan, it has become an important icon and an integral part of the community's identity. Certainly it is still a monument to the Dutch heritage as originally conceived, but it also represents industry and self-sufficiency and reinforces that sustainability and harnessing the wind for power are not new ideas. The mill contributes to the community in a very practical way. In addition to still drawing thousands of visitors a year, De Zwaan produces flour that is purchased both locally and all over the country. Community partnerships have been formed in order to provide flour to restaurants, bakeries, and senior centers, and even cracked wheat to a local distillery for making a Dutch gin. The windmill serves an important role standing over the city, yet is interwoven into the fabric of the community.

*De Zwaan today draws tourists, produces flour, and serves as a backdrop for weddings.* City of Holland, Windmill Island Archives

In hindsight, the city of Holland was quite forward thinking when in the early 1960s it conceived of an authentic Dutch windmill to celebrate the heritage of the city and create a cultural destination that would stimulate the economy for generations to come. In the United States, as in The Netherlands and elsewhere in the world, the 1960s marked a time that preservation was still in its infancy. It is surprising that efforts in historic preservation in The Netherlands, where built environments date back to the Middle Ages, took a parallel course with those in the much younger United States. As it will be recalled from Chapter 2, 1961 marked the year that The Netherlands wrote formal law to protect its historic structures and sites. A similar national policy regarding historic preservation in the United States was written into law only five years later, in 1966, two years after De Zwaan arrived in America. As in The Netherlands, this law came as a result of preservation efforts that began about a century earlier.

The first of these efforts in the United States took place in the 1850s when George Washington's nephew unsuccessfully attempted to sell his uncle's deteriorating home, Mount Vernon. To pre-

*Windmill Island as it exists today.* City of Holland, Windmill Island Archives

vent the structure's razing or conversion to a resort, Ann Pamela Cunningham, a young private citizen, created the Mount Vernon Ladies' Association to purchase and restore the home. The group's effort would serve as a blueprint for later organizations.

Toward the end of the nineteenth century, as the United States was rebuilding after the Civil War, the country began to embrace a sense of national identity and history. Out of that, the government slowly created legislation for the preservation of historically significant sites and objects. In 1906, President Theodore Roosevelt signed the Antiquities Act that "prohibited the excavation of antiquities from public lands without a permit from the Secretary of Interior" and gave the president authority to declare a specific piece of land a national monument. In 1916, the Department of the Interior established the National Park Service, the nation's first agency to regu-

late and manage public space, including national monuments.

In 1935, Congress approved the Historic Sites Act that established a national policy for preservation and permitted the Secretary of Interior to create programs on behalf of preservation efforts. One such program, the Historic American Buildings Survey, resulted in the documentation of historic properties throughout the country. In 1949, President Harry Truman signed the National Trust for Historic Preservation Act "to facilitate public participation in the preservation of sites, buildings and objects of national significance or international interest." Seventeen years later, in 1966, President Lyndon B. Johnson signed into law the National Historic Preservation Act, which established several institutions including the Advisory Council on Historic Preservation, State Historic Preservation Office, and National Register of Historic Places. With passage of the act, Congress finally made the federal government a full partner and leader in historic preservation. While recognizing that national goals for historic preservation could best be achieved by supporting the drive, enthusiasm, and wishes of local citizens and communities, Congress also understood that the federal government must set an example through enlightened policies and practices. In the words of the act, the federal government's role would be to "provide leadership" for preservation, "contribute to" and "give maximum encouragement" to preservation, and "foster conditions under which our modern society and our prehistoric and historic resources can exist in productive harmony."

This act marked the beginning of a period of widespread restoration of significant historical structures across the country, windmills among them. It is interesting to consider that just as De Zwaan began its life in America, fully restored, drawing thousands of visitors each year, the other Dutch-style windmills were suffering in various states of decay; several had ceased operation or had to be closed to the public. The example of De Zwaan as a heritage and tourism site, combined with the new national support of historic preservation, undoubtedly influenced the caretakers of the other Dutch windmills in the United States, as well as windmills of other types. In the half century since the establishment of the National Historic Preservation Act, most of the other Dutch windmills discussed in Chapter 2 have been well cared for and continue to serve as cultural attractions.

The oldest of the American-built Dutch windmills—Farris Mill built on Cape Cod in 1633—has been maintained by the Henry Ford Museum in its new home in Green-

*Farris Mill at Greenfield Village in Michigan.* Courtesy Greenfield Village.

field Village in Dearborn, Michigan.

The two windmills in Golden Gate Park in San Francisco, both built around the turn of the twentieth century, continue to serve as significant monuments within the park. In 1981, the Dutch Mill (North Mill) received cosmetic repairs, and The Queen Wilhelmina Tulip Garden became an added attraction after nearly two decades of fundraising led by Eleanor Rossi Crabtree, daughter of former San Francisco mayor Angelo Rossi. In 1993, restoration of the Murphy Mill (South Mill) began. The San Francisco Recreation and Park Department, to-

*The North Mill in San Francisco.* Courtesy of the city of San Francisco.

*The South Mill in San Francisco, California.* Courtesy of the city of San Francisco.

*Fabyan Mill in Batavia, Illinois.* Fabyan Forest Preserve.

gether with the organization San Francisco Beautiful, hired Lucas Verbij—the same Dutch millwright that the city of Holland would employ a decade later—to carry out an extensive study of the South Mill. Verbij concluded that the windmill required immediate attention. A citizens' group raised $8 million to initiate renovation of the west end of Golden Gate Park, including the windmill. In 2001, the cap was shipped to The Netherlands for restoration, and by 2011 all the work was completed. Park officials are now working toward a similar full-scale restoration of the North Mill. Both windmills are listed as San Francisco landmarks.

The 1850s-built Fabyan Mill in Batavia, Illinois, a windmill visited by Holland's Project Windmill committee in 1963, was listed on the National Register of Historic Places in 1979. It was also honored in 1980 by its selection to be on a United States. postal stamp, one of five American windmills included in a stamp booklet called Windmills USA. (The others were a 1720 post mill in Virginia, a 1790 smock mill in Rhode Island, a 1793 smock mill in Massachusetts, and an 1890 wind engine in Texas.) With the mill's listing on the register came the responsibility to maintain it as it aged, but it eventually became structurally unsound. Local citizens began a campaign for its repair, and in 1997 the Forest Preserve District through a local nonprofit, the Preservation Partners of Fox Valley, initiated a million-dollar restoration project. The Preservation Partners hired Dutch millwright Lucas Verbij to carry out the work. The Fabyan Windmill made its debut in 2005 with a grand reopening celebration and the blades now turn again.

Since the Fischer Mill built in Elmhurst, Illinois, in 1865, opened as a museum within the Mount Emblem Cemetery in 1925, it has been plagued with weather-related problems. A winter storm in 1991 nearly destroyed the mill, and it had to be closed to the public. Cosmetic repairs kept up its appearance from the outside, but later storms did more damage. At this time of this book's publishing, the mill is undergoing a full exterior renovation.

The 1916-built Bevo Mill fared better than most in its first century of life since it was owned and operated as a restaurant by the brewing company Anheuser-Busch. However, when the company merged into Anheuser-Busch In Bev in 2009, it gave up some of its private holdings, including the Bevo Mill. Since then a private company has purchased the building and spent $500,000 restoring it. According to its website, "the main dining area has been 'white glove' cleaned and polished and painted. The Mill room that holds many treasures, the painted tile murals and painted gnomes, has had many local craftsmen and artisans restore them and bring them back to life. Downstairs in the Oak Room and Bavarian Room new carpet has been laid, artisan glass replaced, and art deco light fixtures recreated to match the others." The Bevo Mill is one of eighteen contributing structures that form the Bevo Commercial Historic District that was listed on the National Register in 2013. The listing notes the mill's "wholly unique, romantic and fantastical design."

The Dutch windmill at W. K. Kellogg's estate on Gull Lake near Battle Creek, originally Polder 259 from Friesland with some parts from Polder 261—a hybrid mill like De Zwaan that began its life in The Netherlands—still stands on the grounds where it was placed in 1927 and can be viewed during tours of the estate. Over time, the exterior thatching deteriorated, and the mill was clad in wood shingles. Many years have passed

***Fischer Mill in Elmhurst, Illinois.*** Mount Emblem Cemetery.

***Bevo Mill in St. Louis, Missouri.*** Author's Collection.

*The authentic Dutch poldermolen at the Kellogg Manor House on Gull Lake near Battle Creek, Michigan.* Photograph by Alisa Crawford.

*Volendam Windmill in Holland Township, New Jersey.* Author's Collection.

as cultural and tourist destinations served as inspiration for the development of other Dutch-style windmills in the United States. Since the 1965 dedication of De Zwaan, several other full-size replicas of Dutch mills have been erected in this country, some as city-run cultural attractions and others as private undertakings with the mills serving purposes other than milling.

Shortly after the dedication of De Zwaan in 1965, Paul Jorgenson, who had a fascination for windmills, built a sixty-foot, seven-story grain windmill on his property in Holland Township, New Jersey. He opened the mill as the nonprofit Volendam Windmill Museum to dem-

since the mill was operational, and the blades are now anchored in place. Although it no longer pumps water, the small mill offers a wonderful look at the type of mill responsible for reclaiming so much land in The Netherlands. It is certainly coincidental that the two windmills in America that were originally built in The Netherlands are within an hour's drive of each other.

The success of De Zwaan and the American-built, nineteenth- and early twentieth-century Dutch-style windmills

onstrate how windmills grind grain into flour. When he could no longer run the mill, his nephew, Charlie Brown, took it over and for years sold Christmas trees from the grounds of the windmill. However, as a private individual, Brown has not been able to maintain its upkeep. In 2007, the blades were damaged in a windstorm. Although the dilapidated mill still draws locals and other visitors interested

*The Dutch Windmill Museum in Nederland, Texas.* Courtesy of John Denlan.

in windmills, its future is uncertain.

As a tribute to the heritage of Nederland, Texas, settled by immigrants from Holland in 1898, the Chamber of Commerce, with support from citizens of the city, erected a forty-foot tall replica of a Dutch windmill in 1969. The Texas State Historical Survey Committee designated it an historical site the next year and it operates as the Dutch Windmill Museum.

The town of Lynden, Washington, founded in 1891, saw significant Dutch immigration through the mid-1900s, and in the 1980s Lynden businesses joined together to pay homage to that heritage. Using a Dutch theme, they renovated several buildings along Front Street, which became known as Lynden's Dutch Village Mall. A feature of the mall is a windmill built in 1987 as the Dutch Village Inn, a boutique hotel offering lodging in six rooms within the windmill. At the time of this book's publication, the inn was closed for an extensive remodeling.

Also in the mid-1980s, Cornelis Johannes "Jan" van Gaale, a Dutch immigrant from Haarlem, The Netherlands, and the architect and owner of van Gaale Construction, designed and built a full-sized replica of an authentic smock mill-style windmill in the heart of Dutch country in Winchester, California, to house the Dutch Mill Trading Company. The mill stands forty feet tall with a seventy-foot wingspan. From the shop, he sold antiques imported from Europe and also displayed an impressive collection of old French and Dutch band organs. His son Henk and daughter Anneke have continued its operation as an antiques store. At the time of this book's publication, the shop keeps regular hours.

Developers of the Sierra Village Christian Retirement Community in

Visalia, California, took notice of Jan van Gaale's windmill and borrowed his plans to construct a similar windmill to be a feature of their new facility opened in the late 1980s. A local architect and builder worked to modify the plans to meet building codes and fabricate the structure. The mill has become a Visalia landmark and the community boasts the address 1 Molenstraat (Mill Street).

Three other Dutch communities in the United States drew inspiration from the success of De Zwaan, choosing to

*Lynden's Dutch Village Mall in Lynden, Washington.* Lyden's Dutch Village.

*Dutch Mill Trading Company in Winchester, California.* Courtesy of van Gaale family.

*Sierra Village Retirement Community in Visalia, California.* Sierra Village.

*De Immigrant Mill in Fulton, Illinois.* De Immigrant Mill.

promote their communities and celebrate their heritage by building fully operational, authentically styled grain mills, similar to De Zwaan, that would offer educational and cultural opportunities while providing a positive local economic impact.

In 2000 the city of Fulton, Illinois, dedicated a new windmill at its Dutch Days Festival. Standing nearly 100 feet tall, on a flood-control dike on the Mississippi River, De Immigrant Mill was engineered, manufactured, and preassembled in Heiligerlee, The Netherlands, by the Dutch millwright firm Molema V.O.F., which then disassembled and sent the mill by ship, rail, and truck to Fulton. Millwrights and masons from the firm in The Netherlands traveled to the United States to erect the windmill. Volunteer millers grind grain with a set of millstones to produce a variety of flours, which are offered for sale in the gift shop at the Windmill Cultural Center, a museum built in 2009.

The city of Pella, Iowa, also a community settled by the Dutch, followed in the path of Holland and Fulton when it commissioned Lucas Verbij—from the same firm that restored De Zwaan, the San Francisco windmill, and the Fabyan windmill—to design and build a 124-foot-tall windmill. Patterned after

*Vermeer Windmill in Pella, Iowa.* Courtesy of the city of Pella, Iowa.

an 1850s grain mill, Vermeer, in Groningen, the mill was built in The Netherlands, shipped to the United States, reassembled in Pella, and opened to the public in 2002. Vermeer's stone-ground flour is packaged and used by local bakeries and restaurants and sold in a gift store in the interpretive center that presents the history of the city.

The Dutch millwright firm Verbij also built America's newest Dutch windmill, which opened in the fall of 2014 in Little Chute, Wisconsin, to celebrate that city's Dutch heritage. After

*Little Chute Windmill in Little Chute, Wisconsin.* Courtesy of the city of Little Chute.

As in The Netherlands, both long ago and in modern times, the windmills in each of these Dutch communities in America have become symbols of the local heritage, icons for the cities, vibrant economic stimuli, and producers of stone-ground flour, all things that characterized De Zwaan after its blades began turning again in 1965. Since its recent restoration—after operating almost fifty years in America as a grain mill, eighty years before that in Vinkel as a grain mill, and another fifty years in Dordrecht as a sawmill—De Zwaan continues to produce flour, delight visitors, and serve as a memorable backdrop for weddings and other events. Taking its place alongside several other Dutch-style windmills in the United States, De Zwaan will soon be listed on the National Register of Historic Places. It will have a unique position as the only authentic working Dutch windmill in the nation, and one of the few structures on the National Register that spent the first portion of its life in another country.

almost a decade of fundraising, construction of the 100-foot mill, patterned after an 1850s grain mill in North Brabant, began in The Netherlands. The Little Chute Windmill took three years to build, ship, and erect in Little Chute and cost about $4 million. The Van Asten Visitor Center features exhibits about the history of Dutch settlement in northeast Wisconsin, and sells flour produced by the mill.

*De Zwaan serves as an idyllic setting for weddings today as it did for the family van Schayk in The Netherlands.* Photograph by Abbey Mathews.

# Recipes from the Maiden Miller

In addition to being a premier tourist attraction, De Zwaan is a working mill producing a flour made from wheat grown by farmers in west Michigan. What follows are several recipes that are especially tasty when using De Zwaan's stone-ground, naturally processed, whole wheat flour. An understanding of flour production will make the process of baking with it more meaningful.

The kind of flour produced is based on the type of wheat used to make it. Wheat is a small grain that is categorized three ways: color, hardness, and time of planting.

Color refers to the amount of pigment in the grain. Typically there is white wheat and red wheat. White wheat has a milder taste than the red, somewhat comparable to white and red wines. Because of the milder taste, the white is suitable for a wide range of different recipes because the taste doesn't overpower the dish.

The hardness of the wheat is important when considering what will be made from its flour. Hard wheat has a higher gluten level than soft wheat. Gluten is necessary to provide the elasticity that allows bread dough to rise. Therefore, bread flour is typically made from hard wheat. Soft wheat is used to make pastry flour for baked goods that don't need to rise, such as pie crusts and cookies. Hard wheat is a relatively new addition to our diet introduced in the late 1800s and is grown largely in areas such as the Dakotas and Canada.

In Michigan, farmers usually plant wheat seeds in October or November rather than in the unpredictable spring when rain can make the fields too wet to work. The wheat seed lies dormant during the cold winter, comes up in the spring, grows through the early summer, and then is harvested around July. The grain most frequently ground at De Zwaan is a soft, white, winter wheat that contains less gluten, has a milder taste, and is sown in the fall and harvested in the summer. The fact that it is stone-ground and made from "whole" wheat makes it more nutrient rich. To understand why whole wheat is considered more healthful, the wheat berry must be considered.

There are three main parts to a wheat berry. The outer shell, a hull that is brownish in color, is the bran, which is full of fiber. Inside in a small corner of the wheat berry is the power-packed, nutrient-rich germ that contains natural oils. Underneath the bran is the endosperm, which is white and takes up the bulk of the inside of the wheat berry. The

*Alisa Crawford bakes in her "Crawford" model wood-burning stove, but her recipes are designed for modern ovens.*
Photograph by Tasha Simon.

endosperm is essentially the flour.

With stone grinding, the entire wheat berry is ground into the flour, thereby including all three essential parts of the wheat: the bran for the fiber, the germ for nutrients, and the endosperm for flour. This produces a product that has a complex texture and tastes nuttier and fresher. However, without the addition of preservatives or refrigeration, stone-ground flour has a limited shelf life because of its natural oils, which will go rancid over time.

The beginning of processed flour dates back to the 1870s and 1880s with the introduction of roller milling. A series of metal rollers turned by steam, or later, electric motors, rolled the bran and germ off the wheat, leaving behind a whiter and lighter flour that did not contain the oils that could spoil the flour. The process was faster and more economical then stone grinding, and the flour had a longer shelf life; therefore, it could be exported greater distances. However, speed and economy began to take precedence over quality.

Most processed flour and flour products sold in grocery stores today are made from just the endosperm part of the wheat. Just as a baked potato with skin contains more nutrients than mashed potatoes, stone-ground flour has more nutrients than processed. To the flour connoisseur, processed flour has a flatter texture and taste. All-purpose flour sold today is a blend of hard and soft wheat and, as the name suggests, can be used

*Packaged flour made at De Zwaan is sold at the island gift shop and on the city website in two- and three-pound bags. Just as De Zwaan's miller had a relationship with a nearby bakery in Vinkel, De Zwaan also provides many local businesses with flour including deBoer Bakkerij, Beechwood Inn, CityVu Bistro, Evergreen Commons, Freedom Village, and Coppercraft Distillery, which makes a special gin with De Zwaan's cracked wheat.* Photograph by Alisa Crawford.

with acceptable results for breads that must rise or cookies that should not rise.

The flour milled at De Zwaan involves an extra step to produce a smooth finished texture while still retaining the nutrients. The flour is sifted to remove the largest pieces of the bran. The fine- and medium-grade bran still goes through with the flour. The coarsest bran is then bagged and sold for making other baked goods or bran cereal. The flour is not bleached, and no preservatives are added as commercial mills do. This allows the flour to stay in a natural and minimally processed state that is healthiest.

The sifting process has another benefit: It aerates the flour and cools it after the grinding process. In both roller milling and stone grinding, heat is a natural result from the friction created during the grinding process. Because excessive heat can destroy desired natural nutrients, the grinding process at De Zwaan keeps the wheat as cool as possible in order to preserve those nutrients in the finished product. This is achieved by attempting to keep the revolutions per minute of the turning millstone under a certain level and by constantly checking the warmness of the flour immediately after it is ground. In De Zwaan, the flour falls down a stainless steel chute where the miller can reach the flour to check the texture and temperature of the product and adjust the millstones accordingly. After the flour is produced, it is frozen for a twenty-four to forty-eight hour period before being sold to the public. For longer-term storage, the flour is kept in a large cooler to stay fresh.

Being able to include the entire grain to preserve the natural nutrients in the finished product without further processing, such as bleaching or preservatives, is a slower process but results in a more healthful product. De Zwaan's flour must be refrigerated or frozen once it is purchased to prevent the natural oils from going rancid over time, much like natural peanut butter from a health food store must be kept cold. It can be used right out of the freezer or refrigerator in most recipes. Ironically, roller milling began at a time when there was no refrigeration to increase shelf life, yet even after that convenience became affordable to all, the process of stripping the bran, nutrients, and oils continued for the economics of production.

The soft, white, winter, whole wheat flour made at De Zwaan is ideal for pancakes, waffles, quick breads, scones, muffins, cookies, pie crusts, pizza crusts, and flat breads like chapatti or tortillas. Although it contains less gluten, and therefore does not rise as high, it can still be used for German pretzels and yeasted bread.

Since the eighteenth century, most of the flour made came from soft wheat, and bread did not rise as high as it does today with hard wheat that has specifically been grown in more northern climates. So long as a baker accepts that a bread will not rise as high as it does with processed flour, De Zwaan flour can be used successfully in breads with delicious results. To achieve a higher rise, and lighten the texture, bakers can mix a 50/50 blend of De Zwaan stone-ground and store-bought all-purpose flour.

To get started using flour from De Zwaan, these recipes offer a nice variety from which to experiment.

# De Zwaan Chocolate Chip Cookies

This is a healthier version of a popular chocolate chip cookie. Because less butter and sugar are used, and the recipe calls for whole wheat flour, the cookies are more nutritious. I make these for my son's school lunches, and they are very popular. I am grateful for the help of Sharon McManus of Freedom Village who tested and tweaked the recipe. Now they are popular at Freedom Village, too!

**¾ cup butter or margarine (1 ½ sticks)**
**⅔ cup white sugar**
**⅔ cup brown sugar**
**1 teaspoon vanilla**
**2 large eggs**
**3 cups De Zwaan flour**
**1 teaspoon baking soda**
**¾ teaspoon salt**
**2 cups semi-sweet chocolate chips (12 oz. package)**

Preheat oven to 375 degrees. In a large mixing bowl, mix together butter, sugars, and vanilla, and stir until creamy. Add eggs and mix well. Add the flour, soda, and salt. Stir until well blended. (Use less flour if using electric mixer.) Add the chocolate chips, and stir until evenly distributed. Drop by rounded tablespoon onto ungreased baking sheets. Bake for 9 to 11 minutes or until golden brown. Remove from oven and let cool on wire racks. Makes about four dozen cookies.

# Alisa's De Zwaan Banana Bread

This recipe grew out of a banana bread recipe from a 1959 version of the *Better Homes and Garden Cookbook*. I prefer the older editions because they have thorough chapters on baking. I have been making this banana bread for years, and it has become a real favorite. The stone-ground flour gives it a wonderful texture and flavor. The whole wheat nature of the flour is especially suited for quick breads like this.

**¼ cup shortening, butter or margarine**
**½ cup sugar**
**2 eggs**
**1 teaspoon vanilla**
**1 ½ cups mashed ripe bananas**
**2 tablespoons water**
**1 ¾ cups De Zwaan flour**
**2 teaspoons baking powder**
**½ teaspoon baking soda**
**½ teaspoon salt**
**½ cup chopped nuts (optional)**

Preheat oven to 350 degrees. In a large mixing bowl, cream butter and sugar. Add eggs and mix thoroughly. Add vanilla. In a smaller bowl, combine the bananas and water. Mash well. Add to the butter and sugar mixture. Mix well. Add nuts if desired. Pour into a greased 5 x 9-inch loaf pan and bake at 350 degrees for 1 hour. Let cool for about 10 minutes, turn out from pan, and enjoy a slice warm from the oven.

# Windmill Sugar Cookies

I adapted this recipe from one my grandmother used and am grateful she taught me how to bake cookies when I was a young girl. When I make these cookies, I cut them out with a windmill cookie cutter, hence the name. When we make them at Christmastime, we use all sorts of shapes from the cookie cutter collection. I think you will find, as we have, that these cookies are a delicious way to enjoy the natural whole-grain goodness of stone-ground flour.

**½ cup butter**
**¾ cup sugar**
**2 eggs**
**1 teaspoon vanilla**
**1 teaspoon nutmeg**
**1 teaspoon baking powder**
**½ teaspoon baking soda**
**½ teaspoon salt**
**2 ½ cups De Zwaan flour**
**(Also try 50% stone-ground and 50% unbleached white flour)**

Preheat oven to 350 degrees. In a large mixing bowl, cream butter and sugar. Add eggs and vanilla and beat. In a separate bowl, measure flour, then add to it the nutmeg, baking powder, baking soda, and salt. Mix well, then add to butter mixture. Blend thoroughly. When well mixed, divide dough and roll out. Cut out with cutter and place on ungreased cookie sheet. Bake at 350 degrees for 8 to 10 minutes. Remove from cookie sheet after cooling for 1 to 2 minutes. Cookies may be decorated with frosting after baking or with colored sugar before baking.

# Graham Bread

This recipe is over 100 years old and is provided by Gerry Duke, a regular customer of De Zwaan's flour, who got the recipe from her Grandma Gable. I still remember the first time Gerry and I spoke by phone and how excited she was to track down stone-ground flour. We spoke again after her flour order arrived and she baked this bread. She explained that she and her sister had tried repeatedly over the years to duplicate the bread they remembered their grandmother making, and nothing could come close, until she used flour from De Zwaan. She was thrilled to experience the taste close to what she remembered and has since become a loyal customer and loves our flour.

**1 ½ cups brown sugar**
**3 cups sour milk or buttermilk**
**4 ½ cups De Zwaan flour**
**3 tablespoons lard or shortening**
**2 eggs**
**3 teaspoons baking soda**
**½ teaspoon baking powder**

Preheat oven to 350 degrees. Mix all ingredients together in a large bowl and then melt the lard or shortening and blend it into mixture. Pour into loaf pans and bake at 350 degrees for 40 to 60 minutes. This recipe makes two loaves.

# Pumpkin Muffins

When searching for a healthier alternative to send in to my son's Montessori school for his birthday treat, I found a recipe for pumpkin cupcakes that I converted to muffins for use with our stone-ground flour from the windmill. It was immensely popular, so I have made them every fall since then. These muffins are a delicious way to enjoy both the taste of pumpkin and the flour from De Zwaan. As an additional bonus, your house will smell wonderful while the muffins are baking. Just be forewarned: they are so delicious that they won't last long.

¾ **cup sugar**
1 **cup pumpkin (canned pumpkin works well)**
½ **cup canola or vegetable oil**
2 **eggs**
1 **cup De Zwaan flour**
1 **teaspoon baking powder**
1 **teaspoon baking soda**
1 **teaspoon cinnamon**
½ **teaspoon nutmeg**
½ **teaspoon pumpkin pie spice**
¼ **teaspoon salt**

Preheat oven to 350 degrees. In a large mixing bowl, beat together the first four ingredients. Add the rest of the dry ingredients and stir well. Fill 12 muffin cups (paper liners work well). Bake for 30 minutes until the centers are baked through. Let cool, unless you can't wait to try them!

# Pizza Crust

Kath Usitalo, who writes for the webzine *Great Lakes Gazette.com,* provided this recipe. She visited De Zwaan at Tulip Time and took home a bag of stone-ground whole wheat flour. As she prepared to make a pizza crust, she noticed that De Zwaan's flour, which is ground from soft, white wheat, is softer that the whole wheat flour that she normally buys, so she had to add a bit more flour than usual. She made a veggie and a meat pizza, and her family loved both. "I would count that as success, *wooden shoe*?" she mused. This recipe makes two crusts with four to six slices each.

**2 packages active dry yeast (or 4-½ teaspoons yeast)**
**1½ cups warm water**
**1 teaspoon sugar**
**2 cups unbleached white flour**
**1 cup De Zwaan flour**
**flour for kneading**
**2 teaspoons salt**
**2 tablespoons vegetable or olive oil**

Preheat oven to 425 degrees. In a small cup dissolve yeast in ½ cup warm water mixed with sugar. Set aside until yeast foams. Place flour in large bowl, stir in salt. Add yeast mixture, balance of warm water, and oil. Stir to make stiff dough; sprinkle in additional flour if needed. Flour a board and turn dough out. Knead until smooth and not sticky. Put dough into greased bowl, and turn dough to grease all sides. Cover with dish towel and place in a warm spot (perhaps the oven with the oven light on). Allow to rise until dough doubles in size. Roll out on pizza stone or baking sheet, add desired cheese and toppings, and bake for 15 to 20 minutes.

# Acknowledgments

Writing this book has been a journey in many ways and even though there were solitary moments, the reality is that it was accomplished with the help of many people.

As I reflect on my life, certain aspects included in this book date back to my youth, such as when I began to work in milling; others were turning points that set me on the path where I was ultimately supposed to be. For that synchronicity to occur, people entered my life at just the right time. When I asked the question about milling, *Will you teach me?* Kevin Rogers was there to say yes, becoming both a mentor and a friend. Another mentor, Charlie Howell, a fourth-generation British miller and millwright, taught me the art of stone dressing. I am grateful to them both.

My move to Holland, Michigan, started a whole new chapter in my life. I arrived in Holland fifty years after my grandparents, who came here when my grandfather accepted the position as superintendent of Holland Public Schools. For my own move, I thank Ann Kiewel, past director of the Holland Historical Trust, who brought me here from Honolulu to become the education director of the Holland Museum. A few years later, Ad van den Akker opened the door to De Zwaan by hiring me to work for him at Windmill Island—a major turning point in my life and career.

The chance to train in The Netherlands and become a Dutch-certified miller widened my world in a way I never could have predicted. Many people helped me on this path, beginning with the chance visit of Mark Langerhorst to De Zwaan. He put me in touch with folks in the Dutch windmill world, including women millers Aggie Fluitman and Josien de Vries, who invited me to journey to The Netherlands and train on their windmills. Many millers and several organizations, including the Zaansche Molen Society, De Hollandsche Molen, Het Gilde van Vrijwillige Molenaars, Het Ambachtelijk Korenmolenaars Gilde, and the millwright firm of Verbij Hoogmade b.v., aided me along the way. Special thanks are due to both Wouter Pfeiffer and Bert van der Voet for their assistance when I wanted to undertake professional-level training for grain millers. An essential person in the process of my training and certification was not in The Netherlands, but here in Holland. I am grateful for the help of Phil Van Eyl, who taught me Dutch and helped me work through all the technical material I had to learn. I am glad to call him both teacher and friend.

The research about De Zwaan done

in The Netherlands would have been impossible without the help of Nico Jurgens, someone who cared as much as I did about finding the true provenance of De Zwaan and who patiently answered my multitude of questions. Other scholars who joined us in the research and who deserve my thanks are Ton Meesters, Johan Bakker, Jaap de Vries, Erwin Esselink, and Bas Koster. Piet Groot was also critical to the Dutch research, and he was assisted by Frans Rutten, Gerritt Keunen, Diek Medendorp, and Dutch Mill Society historian Heer de Kramer. My time spent in the archives of the Dutch Mill Society was aided by Jan Klees and Erik Stroop of The International Molinological Society. Erik also arranged for me to interview Diek Medendorp, and I appreciate his patience and hospitality.

The research carried out in Holland, Michigan, could not have been done without the help of the Holland Museum executive director Chris Shires, archivist Catherine Jung and registrar Rick Jenkins, and a former colleague at the museum, Joel Lefever. Geoffrey Reynolds, executive director at the Joint Archives of Holland also graciously provided access to his archives and assistance with numerous images.

I was able to learn a great deal of history through many interviews conducted both in The Netherlands and in Michigan. Thanks to Leo Endedijk for arranging my opportunity to meet Arie de Koning. Others who generously spent time were Piet Groot and Johanna Schmidt van Schayk. I was fortunate to talk to Johanna both here in Holland and in Vinkel in The Netherlands. Local interviews by phone, email, or in person with Maynard Schrotenboer, Del Schrotenboer, Jaap de Blecourt, Diana and Paul van Kolken,

and Holland's former mayor, Al McGeehan, provided much useful information. A special visit to the island by Joann Lahaye Lashbrook and her husband, Kurt, gave me a chance to learn more about her father, Joseph Lahaije, and his experience of hiding in the windmill during the war.

My most recent trip to The Netherlands was in November 2014 for the ground-breaking ceremony of the new mill that is being built in Vinkel. First, I greatly appreciate my invitation from the committee of the Stichting de Vinkelse Molen to be a part of this important occasion. Next, I wish to thank the city of Holland and Windmill Island for allowing me to represent them in Vinkel. The hospitality provided by Rianne van der Biezen, Hans Kappen, Ebert van Wanrooij, and the committee of the Vinkelse Molen was memorable. Many thanks for the chance to be a part of your journey to rebuild the mill and to spend time with the van Schayks, the grown children of the last De Zwaan miller in The Netherlands, Willem van Schayk.

The book itself includes numerous illustrations, many of which are used through the generosity of several photographers: I am grateful to Anne Farrah for her beautiful and unusual image used on the cover and to Deb Neerken, Dan Johnson, Susan Andress, Carolyn Stitch, and the others listed near their photographs. I want to thank volunteer Bryan Dozeman for help with some of the mill photos and Jack van Heest for his excellent work with the diagram of the mill.

Holland's Geoffrey Reyolds, and Craig Rich read through the manuscript and offered valuable input and critiques, and Mayor Kurt Dykstra wrote a beautiful forward. Special thanks to the staff at In-Depth Editions, including Ann Weller for her comments and her steady work proofing the pages. Particular gratitude is extended to the talented editor of this book, Valerie van Heest, who is herself an award-winning author of six books. Thank you for having the vision for this project and for encouraging me to see it through from inception to completion. I feel lucky to have worked with her and am glad that she was willing to join me for the journey.

I could not have written this book or completed my training and certification without the support and encouragement provided by my extended family. For everything from the child care help they provided during my trips to The Netherlands, to the unwavering belief they have in me, I am grateful. Special thanks go to my children for their patience, support, and tolerance, especially to my son Charlie, who helped care for his younger brother, Alix, while I was researching and writing about a subject that I love almost as much as my two boys. I hope that I have been able to teach by example that true accomplishment requires sacrifice.

And last but not least, my thanks go to Bill Wichers for the opportunity to finish the work he started over fifty years ago. May he rest in peace.

*Alisa Crawford has been working in the history field since the age of fifteen, and in mills since she was seventeen. She holds a bachelors of arts in history from Kalamazoo College, and a master's degree from the Cooperstown graduate program in history museum studies. In 2002, she joined the staff at Windmill Island in Holland. Four years later, she began training on mills in The Netherlands, and in September 2007 became the first overseas student to become a Dutch-certified miller. In 2010, She completed a rigorous course and was admitted into the professional grainmillers guild, as the only woman among 35 Dutch men. Alisa has been featured in several magazines in the United States and The Netherlands, including O: The Oprah Magazine. She continues to blaze a trail that is all her own, reaching new heights along the way, and proving that she is far from a "run of the mill" woman.* Author's collection.

# Bibliography

**Archives**

Holland Museum Archives. Windmill Island Files. Willard Wichers Files.

Joint Archives of Holland. Windmill Island Files.

City of Holland. Windmill Island Files.

**Books**

Adex Advertising, Inc. *The Story of the Dutch Windmill De Zwaan.* Holland, MI: City of Holland & Adex Advertising, Inc. 1965.

Balazs, Gyorgy, and Miklos Cseri, eds. *T.I.M.S. 9th Transactions 1997.* Budapest, Hungary: Magyar Molinologiai Tarsasag. 2004.

Besselaar, Herman. *Molens van Nederland.* Amsterdam: Uitgevers Maatschappij Kosmos b.v. 1974.

Boorsma, Pieter. *Duizend Zaanse Molens.* Wormerveer, The Netherlands: Drukkerij Meijer. 1950.

Brooks, Laura. *Windmills.* New York: Metro Books, An Imprint of Friedman / Fairfax Publishers. 1999.

Buma, Peter. *War Memories: World War II as I Saw It.* Grand Rapids, MI: Peter Buma. 2007.

Butler, Jane Benton, ed. *T.I.M.S. 10th Transactions 2000.* Orange, VA: TIMS America. 2002.

De Hollandsche Molen. *Molens: De nieuwe Stokhuyzen.* Zwolle, The Netherlands: Waanders Uitgevers. 2007.

De Hollandsche Molen. *Molenstudies: Bijdragen tot de kennis van de Nederlandse Molens.* Zutphen, The Netherlands: De Walburg Pers. 1989.

De Hollandsche Molen. *Ruimte voor Molens.* Amsterdam: Vereniging De Hollandsche Molen. 1995.

Den Uyl, Paul. *The Holland Fire Department, The First Fifty Years, 1867-1916.* Holland, MI: Flying Owl Publications. 2008.

Dunnigan, Brian L. *Frontier Metropolis: Picturing Early Detroit 1701-1838.* Detroit, MI: Wayne State University Press. 2001.

*Eagle Heights, The W.K. Kellogg Manor House.* Hickory Corners, MI: Kellogg Biological Station, Michigan State University. Circa 2001.

Eman, Diet, and James Schaap. *Things We Couldn't Say.* Grand Rapids, MI: William B. Eerdmans Publishing Company. 1999.

Endedijk, Leo. *Hollandse Molens.* Amsterdam: Stichting Open Monumentendag. 1998.

Hefner, Robert J. *Windmills of Long Island.* New York: W.W. Norton & Company and Society for the Preservation of Long Island Antiquities. 1983.

Hills, Richard L. *Power from Wind: A history of windmill technology.* Cambridge, England: Cambridge University Press. 1994.

Howell, Charles, and Allan Keller. *The Mill at Philipsburg Manor Upper Mills and A Brief History of Milling.* Tarrytown, NY: Sleepy Hollow Restorations. 1977.

Husslage, G. *Windmolens.* Amsterdam: Uitgeverij Heijnis nv. 1965.

The International Molinological Society, *Dictionary of Molinology.* Compiled by the Working Group of TIMS, Yves Coutant, Michael Harverson, Yolt IJzerman, Berthold Moog. Watford, Herts, England. 2004.

Kayes, Lois Jesiek. *Jenison Electric Park.* Holland, MI: In-Depth Editions, 2014.

*Keukenhof Holland Parkgids/Parkguide 2009.* Amstelveen, The Netherlands: KopArt. 2009.

Kooijman, Rob. *De Zaansche Molen.* Zaandijk, The Netherlands: Vereniging de Zaansche Molen. 2000.

Lombardo, Daniel. *Windmills of New England: Their Genius, Madness, History & Future.* Cape Cod, MA: On Cape Publications. 2003.

Michel, Sara. *With This Inheritance: Holland, Michigan – the Early Years.* Spring Lake, MI: River Road Publications, Inc. 1984.

*Netherlands Openluchtmuseum Guide.* Amsterdam: Uitgeverij SUN. 2003.

Peereboom, John, translator. H.R.H. Wilhelmina Princess of the Netherlands autobiography/memoir: *Lonely but Not Alone.* New York: McGraw-Hill Book Company, Inc., Hutchinson & Co. Ltd. 1960.

Roose, Willem. *Molens in Nederland.* Alphen aan den Rijn, The Netherlands: Atrium.

Roozen, Annelies. *Molens / Mills.* Amersfoort, The Netherlands: Bekking & Blitz. 2011.

Sipman, Anton. *Molenbouw: het staande werk van de bovenkruiers.* Zutphen, The Netherlands: Walburg Pers. 1976.

Shorto, Russell. *The Island at the Center of the World.* New York: Vintage Books, A division of Random House Inc. 2005.

Smit, Jos. *Molens in Nederland.* Alphen aan den Rijn, The Netherlands: Atrium van ICOB b.v. 1984.

Stanford, Linda Oliphant. *W.K. Kellogg and His Gull Lake Home: From Eroded Cornfield to Estate to Biological Station.* Hickory Corners, MI: W.K. Kellogg Biological Station, Michigan State University. 1983.

Stokhuyzen, Frederick. *The Dutch Windmill.* Bussum, The Netherlands: C. A. J. van Dishoeck. 1962.

Stokhuyzen, Frederick. *Molens.* Bussum, The Netherlands: Van Dishoeck. 1972.

Van Kolken, Diana. *Introducing the Shakers.* Bowling Green, OH: Gabriel's Horn Publishing Co. 1985.

Van der Voet, A.E., Gunneweg, Jos and Willem Roose. *Het Nederlands Malend Korenmolenboek.* The Netherlands: Het Ambachtelijk Korenmolenaars Gilde.

Van Wassenaer, Nicolaes. "From the 'Historisch Verhael' 1624-1630." Pp. 61-96 in *Narratives of New Netherland, 1609-1664* by J. Franklin Jameson. New York: Charles Scribner's Sons. 1909.

Vierling, Philip E. *The Fischer Windmill.* Chicago: Illinois Country Outdoor Guides. 1994.

**Magazines**

*Colonial Williamsburg.* Publication of the Colonial Williamsburg Foundation. Williamsburg, Virginia.

*Food for Thought Magazine.* Grand Rapids, Michigan.

*Gildebrief.* Publication of Het Gilde van Vrijwillige Molenaars. Netherlands.

*Molens.* Publication of De Hollandsche Molen. Amsterdam, The Netherlands.

*Molenwereld.* Publication of Stichting Molenwereld Moerkapelle. Moerkapelle, The Netherlands.

*Old Mill News.* Publication of the Society for the Preservation of Old Mills. United States.

**Newspapers**

*Chicago Tribune.* Various articles spanning 1965-1987.

Grand Haven Tribune. Various articles spanning 2007-2012.

*The Trouw.* Amsterdam. Various articles spanning 2002-2010.

Vande Water, Randall P. *"Windmill Celebrates 40th Anniversary!" (Special to the Sentinel)* Holland, MI: The Holland Sentinel. April 15, 2005.

*The Holland Sentinel.* Various articles spanning 1961-2014.

*Holland City News.* Various articles spanning 1972-1977.

*Holland Evening Sentinel.* Various articles spanning 1929-1976.

*De Hollander (The Hollander).* Various articles spanning 1851-1860, 1866-1895.

*Kalamazoo Gazette.* Various articles spanning 1962-1965.

**Websites**

www.cityoffulton.us/visit-fulton/fulton-attractions/de-immigrant-windmill.html.

www.dutchvillageinn.net/about-the-inn.html.

www.goldenwindmill.org.

www.illinoiswindmills.org.

www.kaneforest.com/historicsites/fabyanwindmill.aspx.

www.littlechutewindmill.org.

www.molendatabase.org

www.thebevomill.com/history-and-now.

www.vinkelsemolen.nl.

en.wikipedia.org/wiki/Golden_Gate_Park_windmills.

**Interviews**

de Blecourt, Jaap. In-person conversations, February 1, 2015.

de Koning, Arie. In-person conversation, March 13, 2006.

Groot, Pieter. Email correspondence, 2009-2014, telephone interviews, Sept. 23, 2007 and Dec. 14, 2014.

Jurgens, Nico. Email correspondence, 2010-2014.

Kleijn, Gerard. In-person conversation, Nov. 2013.

Lahaye Lashbrook, Joanne. In-person interview, June 25, 2012.

Lefever, Joel. Email correspondence, Dec. to Jan., 2014 and telephone interview, Dec. 14, 2014.

McCabe, Jim. In-person conversation, Dec. 2014.

Medendorp, Diek. In-person conversation, June 7, 2007.

Schrotenboer, Del, Telephone interviews, 2005-2014.

Schrotenboer, Maynard. Telephone interview, January 31, 2015.

van Schayk, Johanna Schmidt. In-person conversation, July 5, 2007 and Nov. 23, 2014.

van Wanrooij, Ebert and Committee of the Stichting Vinkelse Molen. In-person conversations, Nov. 22 and 23, 2014.

Van Kolken, Diana. In-person conversations, 2002-2012.

Van Kolken, Paul. In-person conversations, Dec. 5, 2014.

# Index

**A portion of this book's proceeds will be directed to the care and maintenance of De Zwaan. If you wish to help further, you may send a donation to the Windmill Island Maintenance Endowment Fund, care of the Community Foundation of the Holland/Zeeland Area, 85 East 8th Street, Suite 110, Holland, Michigan 49423.**

**If you wish to help the community of Vinkel, North Brabant, The Netherlands, build a replica De Zwaan to replace the one sold to Holland in 1964, please consider a donation by visiting www.vinkelsemolen.nl.**

*De Zwaan* by Alisa Crawford is the second in a series of evocative stories of Michigan's rich heritage by local historians.

Read the first book in the series: *Jenison Electric Park* by Lois Jesiek Kayes.

**Other nonfiction/history books by In-Depth Editions**

### Aviation History
*Fatal Crossing: The Mysterious Disappearance of NWA Flight 2501 and the Quest for Answers* by V.O. van Heest
*Flight of Gold: Two Pilots' True Adventure Discovering Alaska's Legendary Gold Wreck* by Kevin McGregor

### True Crime
*A Killing in Capone's Playground* by Chriss Lyon
*Off Color: The Violent History of Detroit's Purple Gang* by Daniel Waugh

### Maritime History
*Buckets and Belts: Evolution of the Great Lakes Self-Unloader* by William Lafferty and Valerie van Heest
*Lost and Found: Legendary Lake Michigan Shipwrecks* by V. O. van Heest
*Lost on the Lady Elgin* by V.O. van Heest
*For Those in Peril: Shipwrecks of Ottawa County, Michigan* by Craig Rich

### History
*Old Barns and Country Skills* by Derek Brereton
*Shaping Chicago: James S. Dunham's Crusade for the River* by Thomas Lutz